CATCH THE
VISION
2000

CATCH THE VISION 2000

Bill & Amy Stearns

BETHANY HOUSE PUBLISHERS
MINNEAPOLIS, MINNESOTA 55438

Published by Bethany House Publishers
A Ministry of Bethany Fellowship, Inc.
6820 Auto Club Road, Minneapolis, Minnesota 55438

Printed in the United States of America

Library of Congress Cataloging-in-Publication Data

Stearns, Bill
    Catch the vision 2000 / Bill and Amy Stearns.
       p.   cm.

    1. Missions. 2. Evangelistic work. I. Title.
BV2061.S68   1991
266—dc20   91–2335
ISBN 1–55661–184–6   CIP

"Look among the nations! Observe!
Be astonished! Wonder!
Because I am doing something in your days—
You would not believe if you were told."
HABAKKUK 1:5

This project is dedicated to

Ralph and Roberta Winter,

whose kind inspiration has challenged us
to look among the nations
and be astonished at things
we wouldn't have believed.

BILL AND AMY STEARNS are on the staff of Adopt-A-People Clearinghouse, headquartered in Colorado Springs, Colorado. Bill is editor of *Paraclete Mission Perspectives* magazine and is a well-established author, with ten books published as well as countless magazine articles in print. The Stearns are currently at work on a "sequel" to this book. Their forthcoming *(You Can Be) the Church With a Vision: Integrating Your Ministries According to God's Global Purpose* is a practical study and planning book on implementing a big-picture vision in your fellowship.

Bill and Amy offer *Catch the Vision* seminars for churches, conferences, and student fellowships.

Acknowledgments

Thanks to all the global warriors whose stories are chronicled here—stories all true, even though some are told with altered names or details for security reasons.

Thanks to Ralph and Roberta Winter and Steve Hawthorne for their development of the Perspectives on the World Christian Movement course from which most of these concepts are stolen.

Thanks to our Father for blessing us with such a moving vision of His heart for the nations.

If you are interested in using *Catch the Vision 2000* in a Sunday school class or Bible study, a twelve-session leader's guide has been prepared by Bill and Amy Stearns and is available through the William Carey Library (order line in the USA 1-800-MISSION), Box 40129, Pasadena, CA 91114, U.S.A.

The objectives of this course are to lead your group to:
* *Know* the biblical basis of God's cosmic plan;
* *Feel* encouraged that group members personally have a significant part in that plan; and
* *Do* something individually and as a fellowship to align your personal and group plans with God's unchangeable purpose.

C O N T E N T S

VISION
2000

Something's Happening: Catch the Vision!

*S*omething's happening. Something big and dangerous. And you can be part of it.

You're already exhausted only a few days after starting your global quest for the big picture of what God is doing. You've survived an interminable Aerobus flight to Kiev in the Ukraine and a week of driving, hosteling, and camping-out farther and farther east into what you feel is the end of the earth.

Now the dry, golden sun is setting over Central Asia—no-man's land as far as Western Christianity is concerned. Or that's what you thought. You're seated alone on a red oriental rug in an outside courtyard surrounded by low, whitewashed brick and mud walls. The soundless wind puffs dust into your steaming cup of coffee as you glance at the doorway to the village elder's house adjoining the courtyard. You suddenly feel the odd dread that overtakes the foreign traveler—you remember all the news reports of the seemingly mindless violence that so often erupts in these now independent Islamic countries—Uzbekistan, Azerbaijan, Kazakhstan.

You feel lost in these windswept, far reaches of the planet as the dry afternoon horizon stretches northward forever, westward toward the lumps of the Ural Mountain foothills above the near-dead and drying Aral Sea.

The door swings inward and two white-bearded men in dark gray coats and navy blue brimless caps lean out into the wind, shuffle on thick black boots to slowly sit on either side of you. You feel eerily out of place, as if in a dream.

11

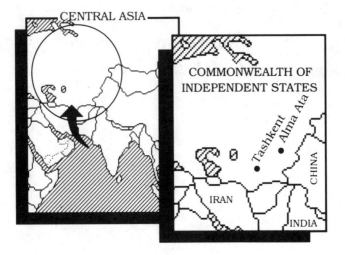

But you're not lost; you're home. At least that's what the eighty-year-old Uzbek leader nodding at you over his blue tin cup of blazing coffee tells you. The other old man, a Korean, interprets for you. "This is where you belong," the old Uzbek elder had said. His dark, watery eyes squint into the sunset as the Korean interprets. He tells you how his heart is rooted here in the dusty plains of Central Asia. He has a toothless grin, trying to visualize your tree-glutted, freeway-festooned homeland on the opposite side of the globe.

"When did you first understand who *Isa* is?" you ask. You've used the Muslim name for Jesus.

The old man nods to the Korean interpreter to tell the story. The key person, the interpreter says, in bringing whole Uzbek villages like this one to Christ is Iosif Vissarionovich Dzhugashvili. You probably know him as Joseph Stalin.

The Uzbek-Korean Connection

The interpreter knows by the look on your face that he needs to fill in a few details.

Thousands of Koreans fled what is now North Korea in the 30's, as the Japanese invaded. Many of these settled around Vladivostok. When Stalin in the late 30's and early 40's began developing Vladivostok as a weapons manufacturing center, he deemed the Koreans a security risk. So he relocated them in five areas around the Soviet Union. One of those areas was Tashkent, hub of the staunchly Muslim people called the Uzbeks. Twenty million strong, the Uzbeks had for hundreds of years violently resisted any Western efforts to introduce Christianity.

As the Koreans settled around Tashkent, the Uzbeks welcomed their industry and kindness. Within a few decades, the Koreans were included in nearly every facet of Uzbek cultural life.

As usual in God's orchestration of global events, He had planted within the relocated Koreans strong pockets of believers. Little did Stalin suspect that these Koreans would not only begin enjoying a wild-fire revival among their own people, they would also begin bringing their Muslim Uzbek and Kazakh friends to Christ.

The first public sign of the Korean revival and its breakthrough effects on the Uzbeks and Kazakhs came on June 2, 1990, when in the first open-air Christian meeting in the history of Central Asia, a young Korean from America preached to a swelling crowd in the streets of Alma Ata, capital of Kazakhstan. The village elder had been one of the first in that crowd to confess to his fellow Muslims that, as the kind, trustworthy Koreans were saying, "*Isa* is the Way, the Truth, and the Life."

Evening is wrapping the eastern horizon in darkness as you cere-moniously spit out the last of your coffee, nod a bow to the parchment-skinned faces of the two old men and head back down the central village road to your LandRover. You grin and shake your head at God's strange maneuverings to make sure every people group is represented before the throne of the Lamb. Joseph Stalin. Who would have thought?

Later you learn a little more about God's odd orchestration of His emissaries among the dispossessed North Koreans. The one million Koreans in northern China, in what Koreans call the Kirim-Song area, are experiencing revival; about 100,000 are now believers.

These Christians meet in small cell churches, and God is equipping these saints in His own unusual ways: A nineteen-year-old girl in Kirim-Song is overseeing a series of cell churches with more than 5,000 mem-bers. And He's providing training materials, funds for Christian medical centers and other resources through Korean Christian networks in the United States!

Catch a Vision of the Big Picture

God is doing amazing things in our world. He's sending Navajo missionaries to the Laplanders, and European Gypsy believers to Madagascar and Argentina. He's shaking up American finances for His worldwide Cause. He blasted open the Iron Curtain and is riddling China and Latin America with a searing spiritual hunger. He's raising a movement of excited disciples ready to go anywhere and do anything.

Followers of Jesus Christ are increasing by more than 70,000 every day—by more than 120,000 a day during the year 1991. Eminent world-watchers sense an upcoming burst of God's power in this final decade of the twentieth century, during these closing years of the second millennium.

Some of North America's most respected leaders are clear in their vision for this decade:

Bill Bright, founder of Campus Crusade for Christ, says,

> We live in the most dramatic moment in history, and I am trying personally—as well as Campus Crusade for Christ as a movement—to focus all of our activities on one great objective: the total saturation of the world [with the Gospel] by the year 2000.
>
> [Campus Crusade's New Life 2000 is] working together with millions of Christians from thousands of churches of all denominations and hundreds of other mission groups. It is our goal in New Life 2000 to help present the Gospel to over six billion people, prayerfully anticipating at least one billion of those will receive Christ, and several hundred thousand will be discipled, resulting in one million new churches being established.

Loren Cunningham, general director of Youth With A Mission, states,

> We are in the most exciting time of all ages with regard to the fulfillment of Christ's Great Commission. By the year 2000 it is possible. Our annual growth rate of church planting is presently at more than 8% per annum. We only need 11% per annum to allow us to place a living Christian fellowship—a local church—as a witness in every community in all the world. We have seen countries like Singapore have a 10% increase of those who have seen Christ come into their lives as their personal Savior. In the 1980s 10% of Korea and 10% of Chile turned to Christ. And over 10% in Indonesia—the largest Muslim country in the world. As we look throughout the world, particularly in Asia, Latin America and Africa, the 1980s was the greatest decade of growth we have seen for the cause of completing the Great Commission.
>
> We need action. We need commitment. It is time to commit.

As Christians do so, we will see every people reached with the Gospel.

"Target 2000," a plan YWAM is promoting, is an effort on the part of the Body of Christ at large to plant a living, multiplying church in every unreached people group in the world by the year 2000. . . . It is a job that *can* be done.

Pat Robertson, founder of CBN and Regent University, says:

We have the opportunity to bring more people into the Kingdom of God during this decade than the church has been able to reach since its founding. It is not a pipedream to feel that we might see "this Gospel of the Kingdom preached in all the world as a witness," and then, after that is done, "the end will come." Because of all the signs of the times, the worldwide evangelization of every people and race and tongue on the earth is the key sign of the coming of Jesus Christ. So are we seeing the fulfillment of the Great Commission? The answer is yes!

Maybe your heart is restless to be a part of His big picture. Maybe you're restless to catch a new vision for your life.

Think over the energy you're throwing into life now—trying to be the best you can be, trying to get ahead, to be a better Christian, a better family member, a better *you*. Why work so hard? Why ask so often for God's blessing on your life?

If it's to have a nicer, happier life, that's not a bad goal. Especially since that's what heaven will be—an easier, better existence. If that were God's purpose for you right now, He would simply take you home to heaven, right? But in the here-and-now, biblical discipleship is never described as "nice" or "easy."

God does want to bless you. But not to make your life easy. He'll bless you because He's got a demanding job for you—a specific task, one that lays down rails to guide your major life decisions, to keep you from spinning your wheels in Christian self-improvement.

Go ahead: Break out of the Christian-culture idea that to join God's family is to become part of a respectable, privileged group. It's more like being born into a family business—everybody is naturally expected to take part in the Father's work.

Do you know what the Father is doing these days?

Look What God Is Doing

If you feel like you are in a dull little corner of Christendom, it's especially critical that you realize what God is doing around the globe today. Here are a few highlights of this final decade of the twentieth century—a period in which we will witness, according to many Christian leaders worldwide, the greatest spiritual harvest the world has ever seen:

- 3,500 new churches are opening every week worldwide.
- 28,000 become believers every day in the People's Republic of China. In 1950, when China closed to foreign missionaries, there were one million believers. Today, conservative estimates say there are well over 60 million.
- 20,000 become believers every day in Africa; that continent was 3% Christian in 1900 and is over 40% Christian today.
- 70,000 become Christians every day in the world.
- In 1900, Korea had no Protestant church; it was deemed "impossible to penetrate." Today Korea is 30% Christian with 7,000 churches in Seoul alone.
- In Indonesia, the percentage of Christians is so high the government won't print the statistic—which is probably nearing 25% of the population. The last accurate tally of Indonesian Christians, in 1979, revealed that more than two million Muslims had turned to Christ!
- After 70 years of oppression in the Soviet Union, Christians numbered about 100 million—five times the number of the Communist Party at the height of its popularity, and 36% of the population.
- The government of Papua New Guinea recently mandated Bible teaching in every school in the country.
- More Muslims in Iran have come to Christ since 1980 than in the previous 1000 years combined. Before Khomeini's revolution in 1979 there were about 2,000 Iranian believers. After years of intensified persecution, there are now more than 15,000.
- In A.D. 100, there were 360 non-Christians per true believer. Today the ratio is less than seven to every believer, as the initiative of the Holy Spirit continues to outstrip our most optimistic plans!

Where the church has been planted, it is growing like wildfire. And as it grows, it is reaching across language, racial and cultural barriers

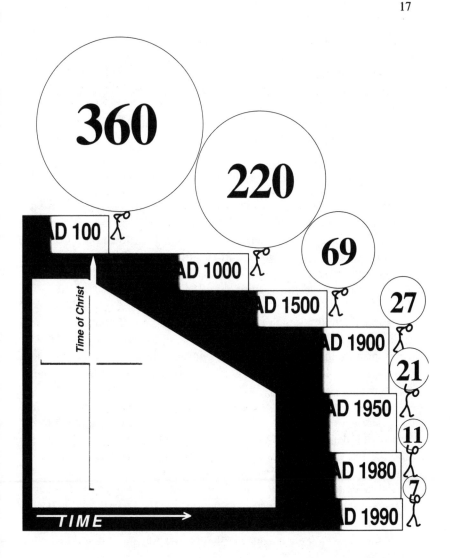

Non-Christians per Believer

Most statistics furnished by the Lausanne Statistical Task Force. Graphics by Richard Endo. From *Missions Frontier* magazine. Used by permission.

to unreached people groups. God has raised up Surinam missionaries to go to the Muslims of North Africa, Chinese believers to settle among unreached Tibetans, thousands of Indian evangelists to target the 2,000 unreached ethnic groups within India. The Good News is breaking loose worldwide!

And that's only the tip of the iceberg of our Heavenly Father's business these days.

Getting a Grip

But, of course, this moving of the Spirit is only business-as-usual in God's historic plan for this planet. As we will see, the Bible has always been clear on the unchangeableness of His global purpose.

Spread out a world map and get a grip on your Bible. By the end of our study together, we will break through to a crystal-clear view of God's strategies, to the specific task He has for you in His "family business!"

But let's think through a bit of a disclaimer first. If you think we're going to scold you for not becoming the first missionary to the Arctic or pioneering through the jungles of Mozambique, relax. Your part in God's global plan may be no more dangerous or bizarre than peeling potatoes.

Think of it this way: Let's say you're drafted into the military. Let's say there's a ghastly war going on overseas, but you're assigned to a processing depot in Toadsuck, Arkansas. You arrive at your barracks and are immediately assigned to the mess hall where your immediate job is to peel potatoes. Now, after a few weeks, it will be easy to forget about the reality of the awesome, devastating war going on in some far-off land. Your major concern is about how dull the knife is you've been given for your task. You get into an argument with the cook. You cut your thumb. The potatoes are sometimes half-rotten. You've lost your appetite.

And you've pretty much lost any sense of how important your role is—that you peel the potatoes that go into the meals that the inducted troops must have to keep healthy, which is essential to their ability to actually fight the enemy as they arrive on the battlefield. You've forgotten the *purpose* of your mundane job of potato-peeling.

All right, so the parallel is heavy-handed. You're doing all sorts of things as a believer in Jesus Christ. Good things, important things. But perhaps you've forgotten—or were never prodded to find out—just how your particular personal ministry fits into the overall purpose of God. Once we clarify God's unchangeable purpose, it'll be easier for us to see just what our strategic part is—whether leading the charge or peeling potatoes in Toadsuck.

So you're off and running in your quest to find out just what God is up to during this critical decade.

You've begun your practical research here in Central Asia, in an area unfamiliar to most Western evangelicals. (Face it: Not many of your friends have been praying lately for Alma-Ata's new Kazak and Uzbek Christians or for the unreached Tajiks and Kirghiz of this region, right?) Before we begin our biblical research, let's send you east into China.

You'll travel by 4-wheeler, boat, and plane across the Taklimakan Desert, into the Kunlun Mountains which force you onto the Tibetan Plateau. Tallying thousands of bleak miles, your journey then brings you south from Chengdu to a remote corner of Yunnan Province in the foothills of the Himalayas. Prepare yourself: You'll be visiting an amiable, colorful people called the Naxi (*naw-shee*) who worship Yama, the god of death.

For Further Thought

1. Memorize Jeremiah 33:3. Ponder the possibilities of what God is planning for you in His purpose for these years of global harvest.
2. Get out a globe or world map and pinpoint the places mentioned in this chapter.
3. Remember that Jesus warned there would be two great problems in the harvest (Matthew 9:37–38). One would be the vastness of the harvest and the other the scarcity of workers. Notice in the passage His solution for these problems. Then begin an ongoing prayer list of big-picture prayer concerns—and be sure to start your list with prayer for the Uzbeks!
4. Share some of the breakthroughs mentioned with friends. Go ahead: encourage your fellow-believers!

CHAPTER 2

The Kingdom Strikes Back! A Twofold Problem— A Twofold Program

Y ou're traveling in the back of a stake-bed truck, wheels buzzing on the only pavement in this part of Yunnan Province, China. Soon we'll hit gravel, so you pull your red bandanna up around your face before the dust starts billowing. High on both sides of the road the foothills of the Himalayas jut up, rocky and glinting granite above the emerald green fields of beans and what you'd call alfalfa.

You whiz past a gaggle of old women struggling under large packs as they head for market. You watch from the back of the truck as they plod along, the sun shining on their bright blue and white capes with silver medallions and tassels. You were told these "firmament capes" designate women from the Naxi people, one of the 24 minority peoples of Yunnan, one of the 54 minorities of China.

That night you sit on the floor of a Naxi house with a travel-weary dozen Western tourists to listen to the men of the village play traditional, wheezing music on instruments that remind you of musical saws. The evening air is balmy beyond the haze of cigarette smoke in the room; the music is strange and mesmerizing.

The Naxi culture is heavily influenced by its ancient matriarchal social traditions; in the past, the women "wore the pants" in the family. Today, women still occupy most of the important roles in Naxi agriculture and horse-breeding. Although the tradition is changing because of the influence of the majority Han Chinese peoples, Naxi families still often live in large households ruled by the grandmother. In the recent past, Naxi women would handle business affairs while the men played a domestic role, caring for the children and tending the garden.

A Naxi couple would live with the woman's family. She could have

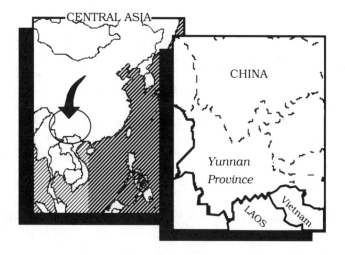

more than one husband, or she might share her sister's husband or husbands in a sort of group marriage. Marriage itself is traditionally very informal: A woman could take a man as a partner or *azhu* for several months, years or just a few days. There is very little commitment in the father-child relationship.

The Naxi worship nature gods in a mixture of Tibetan Lamanism and the ancient Bon religion, Buddhism and Chinese Taoism. Their many gods—the demons—are placated and manipulated with magic and elaborate rituals involving blood sacrifices. Naxi shamans invite the demons to possess them, and while in a trance foretell the future and answer seekers' questions. As you noticed today on your tour of Naxi land, most of the religious statues and idols portray the gods as fierce and terrible as they trample on animals and humans. Among the most fearsome gods is Yama, the god of death. Often linked with Yama is his partner Tsmundi, a goddess who holds a skull-bowl full of blood.

You stretch to relieve the kink in your back as you listen to the Naxi music, suddenly a little uneasy in the blackness of the night outside. You wonder how God is going to reach this unusual people group with His offer of redemption. They have no common written language, no Scripture, no concept of a committed heavenly Father. And how would you handle what in their culture are the nontraditional ideas of a loving, eternal heavenly Father and Christ as the committed Bridegroom? Besides, foreigners are thoroughly suspect and Chinese authorities would balk at a Westerner working among the Naxi.

Then you remember a conversation you had at a rest stop this afternoon. Trying valiantly to act as if you appreciated the cool refreshment of the yellow, fermented goat-milk yogurt offered you by the tour driver, you asked one of your fellow-tourists her role in life. You discovered she's from Brazil.

"I live in Japan," she said. "And I'm a nonresident missionary to the Xiao,[1] a people in a remote province way up in northern Asia. I have to be a little discreet about details since the Xiao live in a highly restricted province. They make the Naxi look like cosmopolitan jetsetters compared to their isolated, anti-Western culture. Two years ago when I started studying them, I found they were incredibly destitute and lacking in health care; they had no Scripture, no mission work ever among them, no Christian institutions such as hospitals or schools, no Gospel radio broadcasts in their language, no known efforts to pray for their salvation. Yet in the past two years, we've seen thousands of them come to Christ!"

You gulped your yellow yogurt. "What? I thought you couldn't even get to them."

"That's why I'm a nonresident missionary," she explained. "I live in Japan and serve as sort of a broker or advocate for the Xiao people who are located a couple thousand miles away. First I got my denomination's prayer circles zapped and in the first year got 500 churches praying specifically for the Xiao. I got them featured as the focus of a worldwide day of prayer and fasting in my denomination. I championed their cause and got whole prayer networks outside my church praying— Youth With A Mission, Christian Communications Ltd., the Lausanne Congress on World Evangelization, and others."

"Then what?" you asked.

"Then I challenged a Christian businessmen's organization in California to negotiate with the government of that province to build a hospital. The government agreed that if the Americans would fund it, it could have a Christian identity and witness. Right now those men are raising three million dollars to complete the hospital. Then I met two Christian nurses from a neighboring country who agreed to regularly visit and teach at a new nursing school in the capital city of the Xiao's province. Each time they visit, they're establishing more and deeper relationships with the health-care faculty and students."

---

[1]Not the actual people group name.

"Hmmm," is all you said.

"And when I started shouting around the fact that the Xiao are a people of 16 million with absolutely no Scripture, Wycliffe Bible Translators stepped forward with a commitment to start translation immediately! The International Bible Society then said they would publish the translation when it's finished and other agencies agreed to deliver the new Bibles to the Xiao. Last year I took another tourist trip like this one to the only school in the world where the Xiao language is taught. And by God's grace I was able to persuade the school administrators to allow two Wycliffe linguists with Ph.D's to enroll in the school and begin Bible translation!"

"Huh." You still didn't know what to say. This wasn't your idea of the typical process of "missions."

The "tourist" went on: "I helped develop an international project team including my denomination's media department, Far East Broadcasting Company and Christian Communications Ltd., to start Gospel radio broadcasts. The real trick was getting a group of my South American compatriots to go on a short-term tourist-trip through the area and record the testimonies of the few Xiao believers. Then Korean Christians offered to make and deliver to the Xiao transistor radios pre-set to receive the Gospel broadcast. Last May the first Xiao radio program went on the air, broadcasting five times a week just as the Xiao get home from their day in the rice fields. They're the only radio broadcast of any kind in the Xiao language!"

Your afternoon rest stop was over and you graciously dumped the remainder of your fermented yogurt into a bush. As you climbed back into the truck, it was obvious that there was more to the Xiao story. "Anything happen from all this?" you asked the Brazilian woman.

"You bet," she said. "Partly as a result of our advocacy, Campus Crusade for Christ has decided to translate its tremendously successful *Jesus* film into Xiao!"

You've heard how effective the *Jesus* Film Project has been: More than three million people worldwide have received Christ as a result of this dramatic portrayal of Christ as scripted from the book of Luke. Guesstimates are that a *Jesus* film in some language is showing somewhere in the world 24 hours of every day. And day after day, thousands are responding.

"With an English-language organization from the U.S., we've arranged that every summer teams of 20–30 Christians go to Xiao land

and teach short-term English classes, witnessing one-on-one to the elite students of the province. Then a couple of long-term teaching assignments among the Xiao were filled by seminary-trained Christians. These teachers found right away that the Xiao are incredibly hungry spiritually, and within a few months they began seeing some of their students come to Christ.

"After just two years," the Brazilian nonresident missionary living in Japan to advocate the cause of the Xiao people located in Asia says, "we got a letter from the provincial capital city. Apparently because of the mix of nationalities in the capital, a church was allowed to open; and the pastor of it wrote to report that a remarkable turning of all the peoples of the province was evident. By November of that year, more than 3,000 people of all ethnic backgrounds had been baptized and were forming small churches. This number was more than four times the total of the previous year. Then we got another letter from him saying that he'd discovered an amazing move among the Xiao. They suddenly had become the fastest-growing segment of the church! He said he couldn't figure it out; of course he knows nothing of this nonresidential mission stuff or the twelve mission groups now working to reach the Xiao. But he claimed that in the past two years the number of Xiao people coming to Christ has mushroomed to more than 30,000!"

And now, late in the warm Naxi land night, with Yama the god of death stalking this exotic minority of China, you almost get goose bumps: Who will be the nonresident missionary to reach the Naxi?

Flannelgraph Religion

The Naxi and thousands of other unreached peoples across the globe have their religious legends. Most of the legends, like the Norse mythologies or the Eskimo stories of creation, have an ongoing theme. The stories usually fit together into centuries-long sagas that tell of a beginning of their people, a storyline that develops their distinctives, and a final episode or two of what's in store at the end of time.

Christians have their own recorded saga, of course. But sometimes believers barely know what's in the record—much less clearly see an ongoing theme throughout the Book.

All too often, Christians teach God's Word as if it is an interesting hodge-podge of stories that are only loosely connected because they all have to do somehow with God. To some Christians, the Bible is like the interesting but unrelated series of flannelgraph Bible stories they heard as kids.

Another common error is to concede that the only relevant books for the Christian life are those of the New Testament. The stories of the Old Testament seem to be like fantasy to some. And the genealogies, tribal divisions, and wanderings of God's people may seem boring and impractical for everyday reading.

Unfortunately, to many Christians, the inspired Word of God—the handbook for Christian life and godliness—is long, seemingly convoluted and disorganized. Is it any wonder then, that some have trouble sharing its Good News with others?

The Book

Like any good saga, the Book actually consists of a well-plotted introduction, middle storyline and a definitely climactic ending.

The intro is seen in Genesis 1–11. The middle storyline rages with wild conflicts, resolutions and climaxes that make soap-opera episodes seem meek—which is obvious to anyone plowing through Genesis 12 to the end of the book of Jude. Then, like any good epic, the Bible has a distinct ending—a conclusion—when all the questions, all the conflicts are finally and satisfactorily resolved. The book of Revelation is a pretty unbeatable climax to the story of the Bible.

The outline described above may not be new to everyone, but what may be new is the fact that *the Book is firmly plotted with a single purpose, an unbreakable thread running through the entire saga*, which has the universe as a backdrop and you as one of the principal players. Let's get you prepped on your part in the cosmic unraveling of God's story of humanity and His usurped kingdom as recorded in the Book.

The first lines of the Book are so familiar to most of us that we're apt to not pay much attention to what they are saying. And they're saying plenty. Whole volumes have been written, mostly in conjecture, about the State of the Universe as described in Genesis 1:1, 2.

Without going into too much detail as we overview the theme of the Bible, let's look at a sketch of the introduction. Like any good opening, it introduces the lead characters and spells out the conflict:

- *God is an eternal King.* The Psalms sing, "The Lord is King forever (10:16); And His sovereignty rules over all" (103:19). He has always been and always will be in full, complete control. We must acknowledge this fact, or we will never accept our part in His great plan. In His sovereignty, He created spirit-beings called angels. He created them in levels of a hierarchy, with specific levels of power and service.

Philosophers reason that God could not create a being with absolute, inherent perfection or He would be recreating himself—which is impossible. Regardless of this view, every being God creates must at some time in its existence make a choice to live according to God's will or outside His will.

- *God's top lieutenant in the angelic hierarchy was an archangel—Lucifer, "star of the morning."* Lucifer ruled God's kingdom in splendor and power (Ezekiel 28:12–17; Jude 9) until his focus shifted to himself. Lucifer decided, as is recorded in Isaiah 14:14, "I will make myself like the Most High." With that infernal vow to live outside God's will, Lucifer became Satan, "The Adversary."

- *The Adversary immediately mustered all the angelic followers he could—a third of all the spirits in heaven (Revelation 12:4–7).* That only two-thirds of the host of heaven stayed to live in the majesty and bliss of God's presence should tell us something about the incredible allure of this ex-son-of-the-morning! With those that fell with him he began organizing his own kingdom, a rulership to counter and counterfeit God's kingdom. Satan established a kingdom of darkness (Colossians 1:13) with a myriad of loyal, diabolical spirit-beings.

- *God created another race of spirit-beings.* But to these beings he added physical bodies; where the spirit and body overlap, the beings have what is called a soul. God created man. Immediately, of course, Satan jumped in to offer the benefits and properties of his kingdom. His offerings weren't opposite God's ideals so much as they were counterfeits. For example: God offered Adam and Eve the fruit of every tree in the garden but one; Satan offered the one fruit that was forbidden. God walked and talked with the man and woman, sharing with them the knowledge of God; Satan told them the forbidden fruit would make them wise. God created man in His own image; Satan promised they could be their own gods.

The Adversary's enticements sounded reasonable and safe;

Adam and Eve were not ignorant cave people. Their brains before the Fall were operating at 100% capacity. (Scientists say modern man uses only about 3–10% of his brainpower.) The first couple had direct access to the whole counsel of God. They could have chosen to live according to God's will, to eat of the Tree of Life and live forever in righteousness and holiness (Genesis 3:24; Revelation 22:2). But they opted to follow the god of death.

Satan appealed to man's natural desire to be knowledgeable and independent. He is still an expert at appealing to the desires and appetites of every human body and soul. "Be your own god" is the latest popular notion today.

And although deposed, Satan is still administrating his kingdom as though he were in charge—wherever human beings allow him to be—working with the deception of the "lust of the flesh and the lust of the eyes and the boastful pride of life" (1 John 2:16).

Satan has organized a global "world system" incorporating both his fallen angels and fallen man. This is the system implied in most New Testament passages about "the world." Things are tough in Bangladesh, in Burkina Faso, in Lebanon, in Peru, in Azerbaijan, in Wahoo, Nebraska and in your living room because "the whole world lies in the power of the evil one" (1 John 5:19).

God's Twofold Problem

At this point in the beginning of time, as they say in the old Westerns, "Things were looking bad for the good guys." God's "prime minister" has succeeded in a coup with a third of the spirit population of heaven, and mankind has fallen into spiritual death and disintegration. This twofold problem presents the basic conflict of the Book.

But God has a twofold program to restore His creation. Part of the program has to do with reclaiming His usurped kingdom. Part has to do with redeeming or "buying back" mankind, who fell under the power of the evil usurper.

This may be a new thought: God's plan is not solely for the salvation of human beings. It also involves restoring His rulership over all His creation—natural and spiritual. Maybe you've wondered: Why did God bother with the risk of creating creatures with potential for evil, like Lucifer and Nimrod and Nero and Hitler—and *me*, for that matter? Why hasn't He completely negated Satan's influence in the universe? Why does He allow mankind to suffer in a world decayed by sin? Why doesn't He just solve everything now?

Perhaps part of the answer lies in the entanglements of the twofold problem. That is, the problem of the spirit world being entangled with the natural world of mankind. In order to restore His Kingship over everything and destroy the power of the Adversary, man must be fully redeemed. Think carefully about Paul's statement in Ephesians:

> I was made a minister . . . in order that the manifold wisdom of God might now be made known through the church to the rulers and the authorities in the heavenly places. This was in accordance with the eternal purpose which He carried out in Christ Jesus our Lord. (Ephesians 3:7–11)

Or think about the strange intermingling of the angelic and the human world in Paul's admission that he had "become a spectacle to the world, both to angels and to men" (1 Corinthians 4:9). The whole process of proclaiming the news of Christ's salvation involves humans and angelic spirits—"things which now have been announced to you through those who preached the gospel to you by the Holy Spirit sent from heaven—things into which angels long to look" (1 Peter 1:12).

Visualizing such activity is reminiscent of the scene in Frank Peretti's book *Piercing the Darkness*,[2] in which one of Satan's servants hurries to his car as the FBI agents converge on him. He is frantic to unlock his car door, but in the rush fumbles through one key after the other, never quite able to line up the correct one with the keyhole. Offering a quick glimpse into the spiritual dimension, the author shows an angel effortlessly flicking the correct key out of the grasp of the evil man. Yes, it is fiction; but it depicts vividly the fact that spirit beings do interact in our world (Daniel 10:10–20; Luke 1:26–33; 1 Timothy 5:21; Hebrews 1:14; Jude 9).

God in His sovereignty is using even the wiles of evil spirit beings—of the devil himself—to further His overarching purpose for man. And in His foreknowledge, He is orchestrating the choices of mankind to further His purposes for the angelic principalities and rulers and powers. The two worlds are intertwined in their problems and in God's program: It's not just that the devil is trying get people to fall into sin; he is trying

---

[2]Good News Publishers, Crossway Books, Westchester, Ill., 1989.

to hold on to his stolen kingship. Sinful man in search of God's salvation is not the only struggle. We are in a constant battle against "the powers, against the world forces of this darkness, against the spiritual forces of wickedness in the heavenly places" (Ephesians 6:12). More is at stake here than man's offensive behavior toward God; more than our own immediate needs and desires.

It's crucial that we catch the significance of this inter-world conflict because it directly affects your part in God's overall purpose.

Until God's Kingship is vindicated and until all of mankind who will be redeemed are redeemed, God uses angelic rebels and human rebels alike to accomplish His purposes. His sovereignty is so infinite that He makes even the wrath of man praise Him and His enemies— including Satan and his minions—to serve Him (Psalm 76:10). In a classic cosmic irony, God allows choice; and yet those who choose to be His enemies in both realms end up serving Him in spite of themselves! According to His timing, God is working to right the problem of the usurped kingdom and the problem of fallen man.

God's Twofold Program

As we might expect, God's twofold program to solve the twofold problem is seen in a nutshell in the Book's intro: "I will put enmity between you and the woman, and between your seed and her seed; He shall bruise you on the head; and you shall bruise him on the heel" (Genesis 3:15). Christ was the seed "born of a woman" (Galatians 4:4) who would be wounded on the heel. And Satan was the "serpent of old" (Revelation 20:2) whose head would be crushed.

Satan temporarily bruised Christ "on the heel" during His death on the cross. But Christ would cast out "the strong man" of this world system (Matthew 12:29). Jesus' death on the cross provided the grounds for Satan's final destruction as well as for man's release from slavery to the kingdom of darkness (Colossians 1:13). He is the Lion of authority to restore the kingdom (Genesis 49:9–10; Revelation 5:5). He is also the Lamb of sacrifice that takes away the sin of the world (Isaiah 53:7; John 1:29). Like Solomon, the most regal of Israel's rulers, and like Isaac who was offered as a living sacrifice on Mount Moriah, Jesus Christ is Lord and Savior—"the son of David, the son of Abraham" (Matthew 1:1).

Christ's Death and the Twofold Program

In the Spirit World

- Christ's death provided grounds for defeat of the satanic counter-kingdom.
- He is the Lion of authority to restore the kingdom.
- He is a regal ruler like Solomon, the "son of David."
- Jesus is Lord.

In the Human World

- Christ's death provided the way for man's release from the kingdom of darkness.
- He is the Lamb of sacrifice that takes away the sin of the world.
- He is the living sacrifice like Isaac, the "son of Abraham."
- Jesus is Savior.

The two aspects of God's program, as seen in the character of Christ, are depicted in one of John's visions in Revelation. After seeing Jesus as the Lamb and the Lion, John hears an echoing chorus lauding Him as the Savior and as the Lord of the universe:

> And they sang a new song, saying, "Thou wast slain, and didst purchase for God with Thy blood men from every tribe and tongue and people and nation. And Thou hast made them to be a kingdom and priests to our God; and they will reign upon the earth. . . . Worthy is the Lamb that was slain to receive power and riches and wisdom and might and honor and glory and blessing." And every created thing which is in heaven and on the earth and under the earth and on the sea, and all things in them, I heard saying, "To Him who sits on the throne, and to the Lamb, be blessing and honor and glory and dominion forever and ever." (Revelation 5:9, 10, 12, 13)

At the end of time, Christ's twofold purpose will be accomplished as He "delivers up the kingdom to the God and Father, when he has abolished all rule and all authority and power" (1 Corinthians 15:24)—referring to the spirit-beings of Satan's counter-kingdom.

We are not involved in this universal scale of myriad events to simply focus on being nice people who do the right thing, serve their community, and go to lots of church meetings—the extent of some folk's Christianity. This is much bigger than that—cosmic entanglements with God's vindicated Kingship at stake as well as the salvation of billions of human beings throughout the centuries. God's plan is not a parlor game.

And your part in His historic purpose is significant, critical—hair-raising.

The Tower

The introduction to the story of the Bible closes—as does any good scene—with a climax.

Adam and Eve had been commanded to "Be fruitful and multiply and fill the earth" (Genesis 1:28). God repeated the mandate twice to Noah and his sons after the Flood (Genesis 9:1, 7).

Why command mankind to multiply and spread over the face of the globe? Some Bible scholars suggest that a basic principle in God's economy is that He receives greater glory by bringing unity out of diversity. If mankind obeyed God's "fill the earth" command, over the eons, geographical distances would separate them into ethnic clusters with different languages and customs. God's epic twofold-program involves a redemption that unifies diverse groups of humanity, and God receives the ultimate glory. In any case, God ordered Noah's sons' families to scatter after the Flood.

But Noah's family decided to travel together east from Mount Ararat and settle together in one place—on the Plain of Shinar. Here they built a city on the future site of Babylon (see Daniel 1:2) using kiln-dried bricks and water-resistant mortar. (Apparently they didn't believe God's promise that He would not send another flood.)

Instead of spreading out in the various family groups to obey God's command to "fill the earth," they determined to build a tower to reach up to heaven—to provide their own way of entering into Paradise. "Let us make for ourselves a name; lest we be scattered abroad over the face of the whole earth" (Genesis 11:4) is pretty blatant backtalk to the King of the universe Who has just repeated His command to, literally, "[swarm] the earth" (Genesis 9:7).

Will God's plan be thwarted? Hardly. God is the eternal King, the Sovereign of the universe. Thousands of years after this period, Nebuchadnezzar, the ruler of this region, spent seven humiliating years playing the Werewolf of Babylon and concluded:

[God's] dominion is an everlasting dominion, and His kingdom endures from generation to generation. . . . *He does according to His will in the host of heaven and among the inhabitants of earth;* and no one can ward off His hand or say to Him, "What hast Thou done?" (Daniel 4:34–35)

Notice the added italics; God operates sovereignly in the intertwined spheres of both spirit beings and human beings.

God's judgment came at the Tower of Babel. He simply pushed mankind into the plan He had had for them all along—to scatter them across the face of the earth.

As listed earlier in chapter ten of Genesis, about 70 people groups are formed, "according to their families, according to their languages, by their lands, by their nations" (Genesis 10:20). One of these families branched out to settle in Ur, near the northern tip of the Persian Gulf. And in Ur is born one of the most well-known persons in history.

*H*ere is where the introduction to the Book closes and the storyline begins. Here is where events become very interesting.

And as you pack to leave Yunnan Province in southern China in your world-class journey, you wonder: What do the Uzbeks and Naxi and Xiao have to do with familiar Abraham?

For Further Thought

1. Memorize Revelation 5:9. Not only does it combine the Lion/Lamb aspects of the Person of Christ, it also focuses on the climax of the story of the Bible!
2. Find Yunnan Province on a map of China and pray for God to send laborers to the Naxi. Remember to pray for the Uzbeks from the previous chapter. (Hard to know how to pray? See "How to Pray for Unreached Peoples," page 195 in the Appendix.) Praise God for His breakthrough to the Xiao people!
3. Jot down your understanding of a "nonresident missionary." Then check with your denominational or independent mission agency to fine-tune your perception of this new approach and to learn of nonresident missionaries you can link up with.
4. Write a paragraph description of "the world system." Sometime this

week explain this concept to a Christian teenager—one of that group who often sees "the big bad *world*" as a joke, as a term for non-Christian people, or as something "out there" that has little to do with them.

C H A P T E R   3

The Abraham Connection: Blessed to Be a Blessing

*Y*ou sit carefully, uncomfortably, on the red woven mat on the floor in the home of an American family, in which you are being served a traditional Japanese meal. Already you're in love with Yokohama, with the fine-faced Japanese hurrying along its sidewalks, and with this Foxwell family of two generations. Grampa Foxy, as the grandkids call him, left his professional magician role and came to Japan with his new war-bride, Jane, back in 1948. General Douglas MacArthur had called for thousands of missionaries to come to Japan, and Phil came to establish a seminary. He and Jane are now retired in California, but regularly visit the kids' families that stayed in Japan.

"So how was the trip out of China? Maybe it'll prepare you for Kyoto!" Phil fairly shouts to you over the laughter of the grandchildren.

You roll your eyes. "Getting through customs in Hong Kong was one of those 'Please, God, take me home now!' times—"

"Amazing things God has done and is doing down there. All those refugees from Southeast Asia—? Cambodia, Vietnam. God brought them out into the middle of the South China Sea in the 70's in leaky, miserable, little boats heading nowhere. Then He saw that they were picked up by the thousands by compassionate ships heading for Hong Kong. Then they were jammed into squalid refugee camps so that the entire international Christian community were practically forced to set up relief work among them. Hundreds of them came to Christ—and still nowhere to go. Hong Kong wanted them shipped out, but where? God orchestrated negotiations to send them home again—only this time thousands of them were believers and excited about evangelizing their own people!

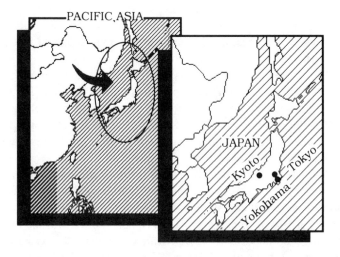

"Almost entirely through these returned refugees," Phil continues, "the first seminary was opened a couple years ago in what used to be North Vietnam. They're openly baptizing in the Saigon River. Thousands of Vietnamese are gathering at 4:00 A.M. each morning for prayer and worship. Cambodians are returning to that bloody country with Good News for their people—"

Jane has to break in: "You never know what God is up to. We just learned a few weeks ago something that went on decades ago in Taiwan. In one year's time between 1946 and 1947, the number of believers on the island shot from 43,000 to more than 500,000!"

"I've never heard that," you say. "I haven't heard most of the things God is doing around the world. I wonder why—"

"Little breakthroughs—" Phil interrupts, urging you to have more tea, "happen so often that Satan and his cronies make heroic attempts to keep believers from knowing about them, because the whole picture would be so encouraging we just might jump in and finish the job. Christians would realize the need to speed up what God is doing—to pull the rug out from under the enemy's feet. Satan realizes no news is good news—to him.

"But about the breakthroughs," he goes on, "when things were still hot between the West and the Soviets, I'd go down to every Russian ship that came in to Yokohama harbor and ask if I could go aboard, do a few magic tricks, and hold a chapel service for the crew. One day a Russian captain said there was no chance I could do such a thing. But as soon as I got home, I got a message from that ship that I was invited to an officers' party the very next night.

"So, I show up and the party is a vodka-drinking bout with all the officers swilling and singing—and swearing—in Russian. The captain acts as though I'm not even there. This goes on for a couple hours till most of the group are falling off their chairs. When the chief political officer literally drinks himself under the table, the captain suddenly motions for me to follow him.

"We go into his office. He closes the door and holds out his bottle of vodka. 'Do you know what I have been drinking?' he asks in English. 'Sure,' I say, checking out the label. 'About 150 proof!' 'No,' he says. 'It's water.' Then he explains, 'I am so sorry; but it was the only way I could get an opportunity to talk with you without the scrutiny of the Communist Party political officer. Now,' he says, 'tell me about Jesus Christ!' "

Later you sit in the night breeze on the terrace with the Foxwell families. "Phil, tell me what you meant about China preparing me for Kyoto."

Phil squints; then the lean, missionary statesman warns you, "The Japanese have had an amazing amount of mission activity in their country for hundreds of years. There are now about 2,570 missionaries here, but the Church makes up less than a quarter of one percent of the population. They can't be called an unreached people since they have the Scripture in their language, and a strong enough church to send missionaries abroad to other cultures. They're the fastest-growing industrial and economic power in the world today. They're smart and sophisticated. But Satan won't let them go. When you tour Kyoto tomorrow, you'll sense it. It's a place where you can *feel* the 'prince of the power of the air.' "

The night suddenly seems chilly. "What do you mean?" you ask.

"You'll see." Phil nods. "Now! More ice cream!"

Kyoto is considered the center of Japan, a beautiful city. Sun glints on the trolley cars limping amid the bumper-to-bumper traffic. Well-pruned cypress and pine trees. Hills circling the city. You sit on a cold stone bench at the edge of an elaborate fountain statue outside Sai Hoji, one of the hundreds of Shinto shrines and Buddhist temples in Kyoto. Nearly 10,000 people in bright red and gold traditional dress daily enter here to worship the spirits of their ancestors—which you know as the spirits of Satan. You're feeling particularly weary today and rest to read a booklet the Foxwells gave you.

On a recent visit to Kyoto, the booklet tells you, Peter Wagner, a professor and author on spiritual warfare, was impressed by the idolatry that pervaded the city. He wondered if Kyoto might be not only the seat of Japanese culture, but the seat of Satan—as Pergamum was nearly 2,000 years ago. "I know where you dwell," Jesus said to the church at Pergamum, "where Satan's throne is . . . where Satan dwells" (Revelation 2:13). Wagner wondered whether the powers of darkness, directed and coordinated from Kyoto, have succeeded in blinding the eyes of the Japanese to the Gospel. The renunciation of Christianity in Japan has been blatant. Meanwhile, Buddhist sects like the Soka Gakkai have skyrocketed from 3,500 followers in 1948 to nearly 24 million today—with thousands of these located in the West. What has all this got to do with the Japanese worship of the spirits?

You look across a white stone courtyard to the Buddhist temple where smoke spews out and mixes with the exhaust fumes of traffic. The huge, dusty, brass Buddha sits, reflecting the glow of the thousands of candles set before it.

You recall Bible passages about "the god of this world blinding the minds of the unbelieving," about Satan's counter-kingdom working to "veil" the Gospel (2 Corinthians 4:3, 4). You know the principle that believers can't rescue the captives of Satan's kingdom without first "binding the strong man" (Matthew 12:29).

The Bible is realistic about this network of principalities and powers and rulers of darkness that hold the people of an area captive in "darkness and the shadow of death" (Luke 1:79). According to some commentators these demonic beings are actually named in the Bible; they are the "powers and principalities" behind such idols as Succoth Benoth of Babylon, Nergal of Cuth, Ashima of Hamath, Nibhaz and Tartak of the Avvites, and Adrammelech and Anammelech of the Sepharvites (2 Kings 17:30, 31). The occult power of these principalities is reflected in previous references to witchcraft and soothsaying (2 Kings 17:17).

Daniel fasted and God dispatched an angel to answer his pleas. But for three weeks the angel battled an entity he identified as "the prince of the kingdom of Persia [modern-day Iran]" (Daniel 10:13). The angel reveals the extent of his battle against principalities and powers as he tells Daniel, "I shall now return to fight against the prince of Persia;

so I am going forth, and behold, the prince of Greece is about to come. . . . Yet there is no one who stands firmly against these forces except Michael your prince" (Daniel 10:20, 21).

Later Daniel learned that the angelic ruler over Israel was "Michael the archangel" (Jude 9). "Michael, the great prince who stands guard over the sons of your people" (Daniel 12:1).

You recall that in Thailand recently a wave of conversions followed special prayer, when the missionaries set aside one day a week to battle the spirits controlling a people group.

In Korea, Paul Yong-gi Cho, the pastor of one of the world's largest churches, attributes the contrast in receptivity to the Gospel between Germany and Korea to the victories in spiritual warfare gained through the ministry of prayer of the Korean Christians. You know that prayer-backed Korean missionaries from Cho's church have recently broken through some of the spiritual malaise of Japan. Within two years of beginning her work, a single woman from Korea was used by God to plant one of the largest churches in northern Japan regardless of spirits!

But you don't like to think about this stuff. The stare of the 40-foot-high Buddha is somehow making you nervous. You suddenly want to get back to familiar things. So you pack up your reading bag and head for something homey—the nearest Japanese MacDonald's.

Getting back to familiar things may be how we feel about thinking through the story of Abraham. But don't count on this being such familiar territory. When we look at the Bible as a book with a beginning, a storyline, and a climax, even the old story of Abraham takes on new light.

The Man

The first eleven chapters of Genesis establish the main characters—God, angelic beings, and man; the setting—earth and "the heavenlies"; and the conflict—Satan's fight for a kingdom and God's redemption of mankind.

God divided mankind into 70 families or nations so the human race could be reached with His blessing of redemption piece by piece; otherwise a unified rebellion against God could again—as in the time of the Flood—necessitate a single, drastic judgment against all of mankind.

The call of Abraham, cited in Genesis 12, opens the storyline of the Bible. The first three verses of this chapter launch the great plot of Scripture that cohesively incorporates all those familiar, favorite stories as "scenes"—Moses and blood in the Nile, David and Goliath, Daniel and the lions' den, the birth of Jesus, Philip and the Ethiopian eunuch and on and on.

Out of one of the nations formed at Babel came the line of Shem, a people who lived "in the hill country of the east" (Genesis 10:21–31) around what we now know as the northern tip of the Persian Gulf. Abraham was probably from the barbarous Chaldeans (not of the later Chaldean empire) or, some suggest, an Assyrian. Today, Abraham would have probably been an Iraqi. Keep this ethnic heritage in mind: Abraham did not begin life as a Hebrew, which simply means "one from across the river"—a term applied to him in Canaan once he arrived as a stranger from across the Jordan River.

In 2000 B.C., God called this son of an idol-worshiper (Joshua 24:2) to go from Ur of the Chaldeans, a thriving city of southern Mesopotamia about 220 miles southeast of Baghdad. And Abram—as he was first named: "exalted father"—became the most widely known human being in ancient history—or perhaps in all of history, since Jews, Christians and Muslims, who comprise a majority of humanity, venerate this man!

Imagine yourself as Abram hearing the voice of God instructing you to travel west: "Go forth from your country and from your relatives and from your father's house, to the land which I will show you" (Genesis 12:1). Now, everyone in Ur knows that if you travel west, you can go no farther than the land of Canaan—an area central to most of the ancient trade routes formed between Africa, Eurasia and the East. Besides, your father with all his herds and servants and your entire family decides to head out with you "in order to enter the land of Canaan" (Genesis 11:31). At least they'll stick with you as far as Haran, since some of the family had apparently settled there previously ("Haran" was the name of one of Abram's brothers).

But God makes this big step of faith even easier on you: The God of heaven announces, "I will make you a great nation and I will bless you and make your name great." You'll be rich, famous. Altogether, this is a pretty reasonable proposition!

Is it really that tough to step out and trust this promise?

Abraham (now called "father of nations") later grew in faith to trust God when the command was impossible. He and Sarah were far past childbearing-age when God promised them a son. "Without becoming weak in faith, [Abraham] contemplated his own body, now as good as dead since he was about a hundred years old, and the deadness of Sarah's womb; yet, with respect to the promise of God, he did not waver in unbelief, but grew strong in faith" (Romans 4:19–20).

Still later, Abraham acted in trust even in a command that was absurd: "By faith Abraham . . . offered up Isaac; he who had received the promises was offering up his only begotten son." How could he even think of acting on this command? Abraham had grown in faith: "He considered that God is able to raise men even from the dead!" (Hebrews 11:17, 19).

But the first call was such a reasonable, astounding promise that Abram had little to lose. So when God said, "Go," he went.

And the first individual called out from among the 70 peoples or nations of the earth struck out to start a whole new people group (see page 198). This would be a people called out from among all the peoples of the world. They would be a people called not after the names of their ancestors—as all of earth's peoples are. They would be a people called by the name of the living God.

Top Line, Bottom Line

The actual promises to Abram pinpoint seven distinct areas of blessing. Think through the passage:

- I will make you a great nation;
- I will bless you
- and make your name great;
- and so you shall be a blessing;
- and I will bless those who bless you,
- and the one who curses you, I will curse.
- And in you all the families of the earth shall be blessed (Genesis 12:2, 3).

These promises fall into two basic categories. First, God will bless Abraham. Second, through Abraham God will bless others. Who are these others? "All the families of the earth"—the 70 families or language-divided nations formed at the time of the Tower of Babel. These were not politically defined countries; the biblical terms family/nation/people refer to a distinct ethnic group separated from other groups by language or culture.

Actually, the second part of this blessing carries the force of a command. "And so you shall be a blessing" could be translated "And so be a blessing." A commentary on this passage by Martin Luther points out that during his lifetime, Abraham personally blessed at least seven people groups. Through Abraham's descendent Jesus Christ, God's blessing came to the Gentiles—all people groups (Galatians 3:14)—as He became the payment "for our sins; and not for ours only, but also for those of the whole world" (1 John 2:2). And, as God later announced to Isaac and Jacob, all of us who are "Abraham's offspring, heirs according to promise" (Galatians 3:29), are to be the "descendants [through whom] all the nations [families] of the earth shall be blessed" (Genesis 26:4; 28:14).

The first category of God's blessing is easily grasped. Sometimes referred to as the "top line" of blessing, it promises that God will bless His people.

Imagine yourself a wanderer and a great king adopts you. Then he gives you his name so you not only enjoy living in his household but receive a royal inheritance from him as your father. Then this great, loving father-king asks you to kneel before him and he rests his great hands on your shoulders. And he blesses you, approves you, vows that all his great power will help you. He leans down and kisses your cheeks and says, "Bless you, my child. I give you my blessing."

That's what Abraham heard. That's what every one of us as believers hears, since those who by faith "belong to Christ . . . are Abraham's offspring, heirs according to promise" (Galatians 3:29). The Eastern practice of giving a blessing is lost on most Westerners; but we can begin to grasp the idea of the fullness of God's blessing on us from passages such as:

> [God] has blessed us with every spiritual blessing in the heavenly places in Christ. (Ephesians 1:3)
> That you may know . . . what are the riches of the glory of His inheritance in the saints, and what is the surpassing greatness of His power toward us who believe. (Ephesians 1:18, 19)
> And to know the love of Christ which surpasses knowledge, that you may be filled up to all the fullness of God. (Ephesians 3:19)

The Book is full of these blessings of God on His people. As more and more individuals in a people group cling to the redemption brought about through Jesus Christ, God promises: "Blessed is the nation whose God is the Lord" (Psalm 33:12). The entire nation or people group enjoys God's blessings!

But the Book is also full of the second phase of God's blessing, the "bottom-line blessing": Be a blessing, and all the families of the earth shall be blessed in you.

Evangelism Versus Social Action?

Some of God's people try to relegate this passing-on of God's blessing to the straightforward task of sharing the Gospel. This is the core, the central meaning of God's blessing, of course, since faith in Christ ushers us into God's blessed family: "As many as received [Christ] to them He gave the right to become children of God" (John 1:12). But handing a tract to a starving man is hardly the fulfillment of blessing the nations.

Others swing to the other end of the pendulum of concern for others and steadfastly follow God's commands to feed the hungry, clothe the naked, visit the prisoners, care for the widows and orphans, champion the cause of the oppressed and the poor. This necessary ministry to the practical needs of people is still only part of the story of God's blessing, however.

How is God's name exalted if a malnourished child receives the Gospel, only to be patted on the head and sent off with a "be warmed and filled"? Similarly, how are we blessing humanity if physical and social needs are met while their spiritual bankruptcy keeps them cut off from the eternal blessing of God's kingdom?

It is clear from Scripture, the Church isn't called to choose *either* evangelism *or* social action, as some have polarized these efforts. Others have paralleled the efforts, with the suggestion that both areas of blessing have the same motivation of love, so they can be emphasized as separate but equal ministries.

But we can move beyond both polarization and attempts at paralleling these activities to a prioritization of evangelism and social action. Blessing the families of the earth with the Gospel of salvation in Christ is received more readily after God's Presence has been demonstrated in a people group through social action. Likewise, following a people's reception of the Good News, social action is a natural result to be encouraged.

Yet how to pass this blessing on isn't really the problem for most of us. Maybe Abraham was like many of us whose real problem is finding the balance between being blessed and being a blessing!

Balancing the Top & Bottom Lines

When God's people focus too much on the top-line blessing, they eventually become hedonistic. "God bless me to make my life worth living—successful, happy" is a result of a nearsighted focus on the top line of God's blessing.

Concentrate only on the nobility and sacrifice of the bottom-line responsibility of being a blessing, and God's people become martyr-like ascetics. They lose the joy of God's family blessing.

Imbalance of top-line over bottom-line blessings causes us—as it did the people of God through the centuries—to falter in seeing the whole of Scripture. For example, how easily we have clung to "Be still, and know that I am God," but have so often failed to quote the whole verse: "Be still and know that I am God; I will be exalted among the nations, I will be exalted in the earth" (Psalm 46:10, NIV).

Why do we cut scripture portions in half to quote the top-line blessings as the people of God? We're familiar with "God be gracious to us and bless us, and cause His face to shine upon us." But are we equally familiar with the bottom line of the continuing second verse: "That Thy way may be made known on the earth, Thy salvation among all nations" (Psalm 67:1, 2)? Balance is critical.

The balance is that we as God's people—just as Abraham—are blessed. And we can fully enjoy God's blessing. But we're blessed for a purpose: to be a blessing to every people on the face of the earth. We're blessed to be a blessing.

The basic balance of this Abrahamic blessing is obviously seen in Christ.

1. Abraham himself was blessed by Christ. Jesus was the Seed of Abraham (Galatians 3:16) in whom Abraham's forward-looking faith found salvation. Christ said, "Your father Abraham rejoiced to see My day, and he saw it and was glad" (John 8:56). The apostle Paul wrote that the Gospel was preached to Abraham (Galatians 3:8)—a Gospel that involved the balance of blessing not only Abraham, but every nation through him.

2. The peoples of the world can be blessed in Christ: "In Christ

Jesus the blessing of Abraham might come to the gentiles [all nations or peoples other than the Jewish people]" (Galatians 3:14).

Abraham's response to the Gospel and the nations' opportunity to respond to God's salvation is seen in the remarkable verse: "And the Scripture, foreseeing that God would justify the gentiles by faith, preached the Gospel beforehand to Abraham saying, 'All the nations shall be blessed in you' " (Galatians 3:8).

*G*o ahead: Count your blessings. Then evaluate each as God's gift given to you for a specific purpose. Each is meant to be transformed through your life as a blessing to every people, tribe, tongue and nation.

For example, think about the traveling you're doing—from home to Soviet Central Asia to remote China and now to Japan. Tomorrow on your flight to Singapore and on to Indonesia, think about it: Why has God blessed us with the miracle of modern travel by which we can be anywhere on earth within 24 hours? So we can have better, more exotic vacations? So Grandma can come visit more often? So you can do business in Baltimore and Berkeley the same day? Or, so we can more quickly reach the remaining 12,000 peoples of the earth that have no Gospel witness.

If you answered "all of the above," congratulations! You're on your way to a balanced perspective of the story of the Bible.

For Further Thought

1. Read and think through Genesis 10, tracing Abraham's roots through the genealogies. Remember that Jewish genealogies often skipped whole generations, going from "famous" ancestor to "famous" ancestor.

2. Trace on a Bible map Abraham's route from Ur to Haran to Canaan. What peoples did Abraham have contact with in that migration?

3. Make a list of your "top-line" blessings—the big and small blessings God has brought into your life. Then, next to each top-line blessing, write a corresponding "bottom-line" blessing—a way in which you can pass on some of God's goodness to others.

   For example, if God has given you a talent as a musician, you can pass some of that blessing on to others by volunteering to play hymns at a nearby rest home or other facility.

   Blessing others in your own people group is necessary and fulfilling. But a tougher challenge is to go over your top-line blessings list and determine how to pass on some of that blessing to *another people group*!

4. Pray for the people of Japan. Remember that most researchers say the Japanese are a "reached" group since they have Scripture and solid churches within their culture. But the stranglehold Satan has over this wise and practical people means that, as a strategic people group, they deserve millions of hours of believers' intercessory prayer!

5. Share the top-line/bottom-line concept with a friend. Don't push the bottom-line responsibility to bless every people as your chance to dump guilt on your friend, but challenge him or her to help you in realizing your own top-line/bottom-line blessings as suggested above.

CHAPTER 4

The Master's Plan: God's Unchangeable Purpose

VISION 2000

Y ou awake, ears still buzzing from the prop-jet flight you endured from Tokyo to Singapore. Swinging back the white curtains of your 37th-floor hotel room, you survey the bright, bustling city-state and shake your head about the newspaper article you read at the airport last night. The reporter decried that so many people were becoming Christians in Singapore that other religions had better step up their proselytizing or all of Singapore would soon be Christian!

At breakfast on a patio near the hotel pool, you begin chatting with an older American couple. She introduces herself as Mertie; she's everyone's grandmother—hair in a gray bun, sweet smile and all. He's Ernie, distinguished with an impeccable white mustache. You find they're experts on Southeast Asia, a result of decades of work as missionaries to the Meo people in Laos—called the Hmong in Vietnam, Thailand and China.

Under the brilliant patio sunshine, over your eggs Benedict, you're briefed on how God determined it was time to bless the Meo.

It was May 1950. Disappointed with lack of results, a missionary family trying to reach the Meo left their village for a mission conference in Vietnam. They asked Kheng, a young Khmu tribesman from the province of Luang Prabang, to oversee their house while they were away. Kheng, a believer "foreign" to the Meo, was a zealous Christian and immediately went about the village telling about Christ.

On several occasions, Kheng noticed a weather-worn old man dressed in the traditional garb of a Meo shaman listening intently to his stories of Jesus and the God who sent Him. One afternoon Bo-Si, the shaman, motioned for Kheng. He nodded and said that years before, a

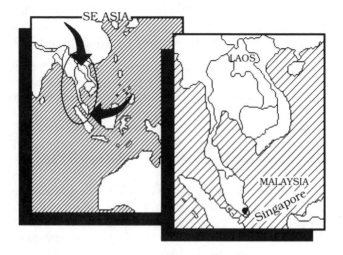

woman shaman in another Meo village had prophesied that in three years a man would come to tell their people about the True God.

"I am convinced," said Bo-Si, "that you, Kheng, are the one prophesied about. And this *Yesu* of whom you speak is Fua-Tai, the Lord. He is the One sent by the One True God!"

Kheng was taken by Bo-Si to his village, where the chief led the entire group to express faith in *Fua-Tai Yesu* (the Lord Jesus in the Meo language). Kheng was then taken to the village of the woman shaman who had three years earlier made the prediction of his coming. After listening to Kheng's story, she declared emphatically that this was indeed the One True God, and led her entire village in professing Jesus.

Soon other villages in the area, who also knew of the prophecy, sent for Kheng, and for weeks he traveled about almost constantly, relating the simple events of Christ's life and the means of salvation through faith in Him.

After being delayed several weeks by a typhoon, the missionary and his family finally returned and were astonished to find nearly 1,000 Meo professing a belief in Christ!

You're fascinated by this world-class couple who look as if they belong home on an Iowa farm. "Is Laos where you began working with the Meo?" you ask.

Ernie leans back in the white patio chair and smiles. Apparently you've asked the right question. For another five minutes you are again amazed at the way God works to accomplish His unchangeable purpose to reach every people in every corner of the world. Ernie tells his story:

Another fellow and I were doing some exploratory traveling in remote Thailand in an area where these Meo or Hmong people lived. Generally the people were friendly and would readily accept us strangers into their village and give us a night of entertainment. We were handicapped because we didn't know Thai very well; my partner knew it better than I, but still he wasn't very fluent. I knew some Chinese and the Hmong knew a little Chinese, but it was hard to communicate.

We came to a village and went to the head man's house. He received us very graciously and many people from the village came to his house to see us. Many had never seen a white man before, particularly the women. They listened, but I am sure they were confused as to what we were talking about because of our broken Thai and Chinese. But we did get across a message about the God of creation and that Jesus Christ was our Savior.

They let us sleep there that night, beneath the god-shelf in their home. The next morning they woke us fairly early and wanted us to follow them. So, not knowing where they were going to take us, we bundled up our bedding and were taken to a new section of the village—new, good-sized homes stood amid the stumps of freshly cut jungle trees. We were taken inside one of the homes. They put out the woven bamboo mats, brought us tea, and soon crowds came and filled the room. Dzunga, the head of the home said, "Now, tell us more about this Jesus that you were talking about. We want to know more about this person."

So, between the two of us, we told them about Jesus the best we could throughout the day—starting in Genesis and going right on through to Revelation! They seemed to become more and more interested as our story progressed.

They asked us to stay overnight. And the next night. And the next. Finally, after a week, they told us that a group of them wanted to become Christians! This was quite unexpected since our language skills were so poor; and on a first trip it is unusual to have that kind of response. But they asked us what they needed to do, and we told them to first get rid of their spirit-worshiping articles and fetishes— to take them out of their houses and burn them.

After they accepted Jesus, they wanted to know what else they should do.

We taught them how to pray, and sang a few songs with them. Then they asked how they were to live this new way, and would someone come to teach them? Would we come to live with them and teach them?

On the spot I had to make a decision. Mertie and the children— under two years of age—were too far away through the jungle to consult. I said, "Yes."

And so we began the work among the Meo or Hmong of Thailand, and the result is seen in thousands of believers in Thailand today.

But why were we so warmly received?

Months later we found out that the man Dzunga who had opened his home to us had a son named Doong who a few years earlier had almost died. The whole village had done everything they could to appease their gods, yet the boy was not healed. A broken, desperate Dzunga remembered hearing of a very powerful God, Yesu, from someone somewhere—possibly from a trader in Laos. The father prayed to Him: "If you are a God who has power, heal my son!"

Doong was healed!

Dzunga and the entire people were amazed at this strong Spirit, but had no idea how to worship Him. Then, several years later, we "big-noses" come stumbling into his village proclaiming the name of Yesu—the eternal One, the Savior of love.

You nod at Ernie's story. "Must feel pretty good to have fit so nicely into what God was doing at the time, hmmm?"

Ernie nods and Mertie smiles.

And you sit, gazing out at the glitzy city of Singapore, sipping your guava juice and thinking about how you fit into what God is doing today.

God is blessing people group after people group. Usually in unusual ways. How often do we have to hear amazing stories of God's breakthroughs to various people groups of the earth to get the idea that He meant business about His promise to Abraham? He promised to bless His people and through them bless every people of the earth, and over and over through the centuries God has been doing exactly that. Have we even noticed?

Repeated Repetitions

The story is told of Carl Sandburg, the great American poet, who as a college student took his roommate home to visit for the holidays.

As Carl introduced his roommate to his hard-of-hearing aunt, he announced, "Auntie, I want you to meet my roommate, Al Specknoodle!" The aunt cupped her ear and shook her head. Carl tried again: "I want you to meet my roommate Al Specknoodle!" The aunt frowned and shook her head again. Carl sputtered and shouted, "Al Specknoodle! My roommate!" Finally the aunt burst into tears; "It's no use, Carl," she said. "No matter how many times you say it, it still sounds like . . . Al Specknoodle!"

No matter how many times or how obviously God has announced His clear purpose on earth to bless every people, it seems His people never quite get the message. We keep thinking that the "bottom-line" part of the promise isn't as important as the "top line," which has to do with blessing us, His people. And, of course, we are more important than they, right?

God knows our dullness of hearing. So He very meticulously repeats His twofold promise a full five times in the book of Genesis.

As God was about to destroy Sodom and Gomorrah, He said, "Abraham will surely become a great and mighty nation, and in him all the nations of the earth will be blessed" (Genesis 18:18).

Then God again repeated the promise after Abraham's offering of his son Isaac—who was the initial fulfillment of the promise: "By Myself I have sworn, declares the Lord, because you have done this thing . . . indeed I will greatly bless you . . . and in your seed all the nations of the earth shall be blessed" (Genesis 22:16–18).

So far God has added the adverbs "surely" and "indeed." It sounds like He means business. Later God repeats the promise to Isaac: "I will multiply your descendants . . . and by your descendants all the nations of the earth shall be blessed" (Genesis 26:4). Not only would the Seed of Abraham, Jesus Christ himself (see Galatians 3:14, 16), shed His blood to offer blessing to the peoples of the earth; also all the descendants of Abraham and Isaac would bless the nations. Who are these descendants? The New Testament is clear:

- The children of the promise are regarded as descendants (Romans 9:8).
- You, brethren [Galatian believers from non-Jewish peoples], like Isaac are children of promise (Galatians 4:28).
- If you belong to Christ, then you are Abraham's offspring, heirs according to promise (Galatians 3:29).

Jot it down somewhere obvious, where it can be seen repeatedly throughout the day—We who belong to Christ fit precisely into God's repeated promise that by us—Abraham's and Isaac's descendants by faith—all the nations of the earth shall be blessed!

Then God again repeated His promise to Jacob in his dream while he slept on a rock-pillow at Bethel: "Your descendants shall also be like the dust of the earth . . . and in you and in your descendants shall all the families of the earth be blessed. And behold, I am with you . . ." (Genesis 28:14, 15).

Have you ever wondered why the Bible so often identifies the Lord as the God of "Abraham, Isaac and Jacob?" If you search the biographies of these men's lives, you see that the reason cannot be based on their sterling righteousness or faultless behavior. Wouldn't it make more sense for God to identify himself as the God of more spectacular figures such as Enoch, Elijah or John the Baptist?—the God of Moses, David and Jeremiah?

But God is the God of Abraham, Isaac and Jacob because it was to these three that the bedrock, twofold promise was given. That's how important the "blessed to be a blessing" principle is: God wanted His name identified with it.

Eventually Abraham, Isaac and Jacob will actually see both levels of God's promise fulfilled: They will sit down at a great banquet and "many shall come from east and west and recline at the table with Abraham, Isaac and Jacob" (Matthew 8:11). Luke adds that these will come not only from east and west but from north and south as well (Luke 13:29)—from every possible direction on the globe! Our God is the God of Abraham, Isaac and Jacob because it was to these men He gave His promise to redeem some from every people, tribe, tongue and nation.

But we skipped over something a little astounding: God swore.

We may think it is only from the mouth of a carnal Christian that we would ever hear a determined, "By God, I'm going to . . ." When a person means business, it almost seems natural in any language to swear "by the gods."

When God means business, He of course can swear by no name greater than His own. So to shockingly underscore His determination, God himself swears to Abraham, "By Myself I have sworn . . . indeed I will greatly bless you . . . and in your seed all the nations of the earth shall be blessed, because you have obeyed my voice" (Genesis 22:16–18).

The writer of Hebrews picks up on this amazing incident and tells us it can be the most encouraging thing that we can hold on to in our helter-skelter lives on earth. God's sworn promise to Abraham can help us to "show the same diligence so as to realize the full assurance of hope until the end" (Hebrews 6:11).

To most of us believers, the topic of assurance usually prompts us to reaffirm our personal commitment to Christ for salvation. If you sense a lack of assurance, you probably aren't certain you're headed for heaven. So the counsel given is almost always to make sure you've made that specific commitment to Jesus Christ as your personal Lord and Savior. And that process does bring a sense of assurance.

But the writer of Hebrews is talking about an even more effective assurance—"strong encouragement [for us] who have fled for refuge in laying hold of the hope set before us. This hope we have as an anchor of the soul, a hope both sure and steadfast" (Hebrews 6:18, 19).

What brings that "anchor-in-the-soul" kind of assurance in our lives? How do we sense that stability? Think through the verses between the verse on "full assurance" (6:11) and the one about "hope both sure and steadfast" (6:19).

"When God made the promise to Abraham, since He could swear by no one greater, He swore by Himself saying, 'I will surely bless you and I will surely multiply you' " (Hebrews 6:13, 14). God promised that *by Himself* He would bless Abraham with an heir. And did He come through with His promise?

"Thus, having patiently waited, [Abraham] obtained the promise" (Hebrews 6:15). It's a pretty simple formula: God swears to do something, Abraham believes Him, and the promise is fulfilled. Looking back on that pattern later must have brought Abraham great assurance that God was indeed—even when things were biologically impossible— going to come through for him. He could count on God. And so Abraham lived another full 75 years in solid hope, "breathed his last and died in a ripe old age, an old man and satisfied with life" (Genesis 25:8).

Why do we often worry about whether God will come through for us? Why can't we spend the "last" 75 years of our lives in solid confidence of His working in our lives and feel deeply satisfied with life? Perhaps because somehow we've gotten the idea that God is supposed to respond to our pleas and needs. And often He doesn't. We become disappointed with Him and—perhaps without ever hinting at such blasphemy—feel that He's unreliable. The prophet Jeremiah felt exactly that way in his life of troubles; he complained to God, "Wilt Thou be to me like a deceptive stream with water that is unreliable?" (Jeremiah 15:18). The King James Version of that passage puts it about as strong as a translator would dare when speaking to God: "Wilt thou be altogether unto me as a liar?"

The television mogul Ted Turner, raised in a Christian environment, points back to a specific event that convinced him God—if God exists at all—is unreliable. As a teenager, Turner prayed and prayed that God would heal his terminally ill sister; but the sister died. From that point on, Turner lived the life of the practical atheist, a role many people who still "believe" in God ensue. They know He exists, but they frankly don't trust Him with their lives because He has "let them down."

But maybe it's time for us to get scriptural in our expectations of God's reliability. He won't always do what we say He should do. But He will always do exactly what He says He will do. And on this we can base a whole new life of confident assurance, of encouraging hope. God will do what He set out to do, and as we align with that, we have steadfastness and sureness like an anchor in the soul.

So what has God said He would do?

He said He would give Abraham an heir; and He did.

Now look carefully at the second solid, unchangeable thing God swore He would do:

> In the same way God, desiring even more to show to the heirs of the promise the unchangeableness of His purpose, interposed with an oath, in order that by two unchangeable things, in which it is impossible for God to lie, we may have strong encouragement. . . . (Hebrews 6:17–18)

The first unchangeable thing God swore about was that He would bless Abraham with a son. That was the basis of Abraham's patient, confident hope. The second unchangeable thing God swore about was that He would through Abraham's heirs bless every people group on the face of the earth. Four thousand years ago, it's as if God swore, "By God, I will bring My salvation to the Meo people in Laos, the Hmong in Vietnam, Thailand and China." His offer of blessing to the Meo was not a matter of "if" but of "when, how and through whom."

God's promise was twofold, and He swore that He would accomplish both parts of His covenant. He wanted to convince Abraham of

His blessing, and yet He desires even more to show to us believers—
the heirs of the promise (Galatians 3:29)—that He will through us bless
all the nations.

His twofold program is unchangeable. He wants us to be assured of
"the unchangeableness of His purpose." That we are blessed to be a
blessing to every people group comprises "two unchangeable things."
And as we align our worldview and our lives with that solid-as-a-rock
purpose, we will have an uncanny confidence in Him, a goal to look
forward to with hope that is "steadfast and sure."

*I*magine that you step on a train bound for Bucksnort, Tennessee. The
tracks under your coach run nowhere but straight into Bucksnort. The
train will stop in Bucksnort at the end of its run. You overheard the
engineer swear to the railroad owner himself that "By God, we're going
to Bucksnort!" Even if you don't know the territory, even if you're not
quite sure of the way to Bucksnort yourself, even if there seems to be
a lot of stops and starts and clanging and black nights along the way,
couldn't you relax a bit with a sense of assurance that you would eventually arrive in Bucksnort? (Yes, it's an actual town in Tennessee!)

Relax. Slip into your own niche in God's big-picture plan of blessing
every nation with the news of redemption in Christ. The way might
involve periods of darkness, discomfort, irritation and impatience. But
as you align your life with God's unchangeable purpose to be blessed
and in turn to bless the nations, you know where you're going. You
know what He's doing. You can go confidently about your Father's
business.

Go ahead. Realize the full assurance of hope. Have a good dose of
strong encouragement. Lay hold of the hope that is set before you.
Sense that anchor in your soul. Enjoy a hope sure and steadfast. Finish
your guava juice poolside at your Singapore hotel. And catch your
freighter bound for Jakarta.

For Further Thought

1. Meditate on Hebrews 6:11–18. Dwell on the implications of God
   declaring His unchangeable purpose—His twofold promise to (1)
   bless Abraham and his descendants and (2) through them bless every
   people group. How can these "two unchangeable things" on which
   God staked His own name become your own sure and steadfast

"anchor of the soul"? If this were the focus of your life, your church or fellowship, what changes might you see? Make a list.
2. Find Laos on a map.
3. Since the Lord has given us a steadfast hope, praise Him for His faithfulness to fulfill His promise. Pray for the Meo Christians who are going out to neighboring tribes to share the Great News of *Fua-Tai Yesu*.
4. Share the encouragement of having hope beyond personal salvation with a friend who is struggling with purpose in life.

VISION 2000

So You're Entering the Priesthood! The Obligation and The Opportunity

*I*t's early morning, but you're sweltering in the green concrete airport waiting area in Jakarta, Indonesia. Ceiling fans whirl in palsied rattles above the hundred or so glowing brown faces patiently watching through the streaked, tinted windows for the incoming DC–10. Dozens of children scurry and chatter happily in elaborate games between the rows of quiet adults.

You unload your suitcase, backpack and plastic bag of curios from Uzbekistan, Naxi land and Japan onto the green tile floor, and settle into a sticky plastic orange chair across from a young man dressed in a sharply pressed black suit. In spite of the fans overhead, the air hangs heavy with curry, disinfectant and the acrid, metallic smell of perspiration.

You smile and attempt to communicate with typically foreign, amplified gestures to the young man: You wipe your forehead, roll your eyes and say loudly, "Whew!"

He raises one eyebrow. "Are you slightly warm this morning?" he asks in an impeccable British accent.

In the ensuing conversation you learn that Pono Lubis is a tax assessor from Bawean, one of the 10,000 islands that make up Indonesia. He speaks English from years of schooling in London, Indonesian—a language derived from Malay and designated the national language in the 1920's—and of course Bawean.

Isolated 90 miles out in the Java Sea, Bawean is a tropical paradise island known, Pono says, as "the island of women." There are few men since most young men leave the island in search of jobs on the big islands of Java and Sumatra.

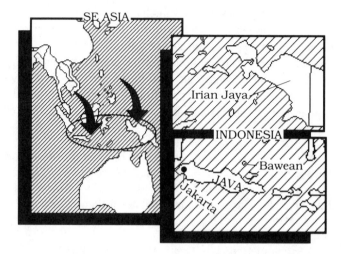

"Any Christians on the island?" you ask.

He raises an eyebrow and sizes you up. "No. Never. We are Muslims." From under his arm he flips out a newspaper and opens it, dismissing you with: "Christians. On Bawean? Hah."

You settle back into the orange seat, certain you've committed some unpardonable cross-cultural *faux pas*. You know that Christianity has been spreading like wildfire among the islands of Indonesia, that although the Islamic government won't print the statistics, one of four Indonesians is a believer in Christ. But there must be some pretty obstinate pockets of resistance—whole people groups that reject the Gospel in favor of a mix of Islam and animistic spirit worship. Like the Baweans.

But then you remember a basic briefing you received before embarking on this wild quest to catch a global vision. Westerners often label peoples "resistant" when the truth is more likely that they've never been exposed to Christianity. Are Indonesian Muslims resistant to the Good News? Have we ever gone to find out?

With no other travelers to talk to, you pull out your *Walkman*, headphones, and a cassette given you by a Japanese couple in Tokyo. They had just returned from a short-term medical team ministry in Irian Jaya, the Indonesian half of the island once called New Guinea. Sponsored by a Philippine Christian relief organization, the Japanese couple were shocked when they learned firsthand of dozens of former head-hunting tribes who have recently come to Christ and are now sending their own missionaries to former enemies.

Dutch missionaries have often been the facilitators for these people movements to Christ, and your cassette player now hisses with the heavily accented lilt of a missionary from the Netherlands who tells the remarkable story of the cannibalistic Nipsan of the highlands of Irian Jaya, Indonesia:

> Nipsan was the nearest village to where the missionaries decided to build an airstrip. So we called the whole area "Nipsan."
>
> In the early 70's we had several close calls. My dad had started a school with the help of the Indonesian government, and the boys who went to the school began acting like big-shots around the chiefs of the villages in that area.
>
> A group of Christians from what we call "Pass Valley"—its actual name is Abanoho—came to work as missionaries to the Nipsan with my father. A point of contention was the difference in the way each group slaughtered their pigs. The Nipsan whisper in the pig's ear first, then shoot it with arrows, and cook it. The Abanoho Christian workers didn't whisper anything to the pig, and they burned off the hair before the pig was cooked. As a result, the Nipsan thought there were evil pig spirits in the villages. This and other differences built up between them over the years.
>
> During the month of May 1974, when we were back in Holland, the head chief of the villages laid a plan. Each village would invite one of the Abanoho evangelists to visit and then they would kill and eat them. Christians who went out to the villages tried to defend themselves, but a total of 14 evangelists were killed and eaten. Many wives and children were also involved in the massacre. Because they weren't Western missionaries, you probably never heard of the tragedy.
>
> Saboonwarek, one of the believers from Pass Valley, just happened to be away at the time. When my dad returned four years later, he asked Saboonwarek if he wanted to go back to Nipsan.
>
> He said, "No, but I have to go back because God is calling me there."
>
> Saboonwarek is back in Nipsan now, and he is the key man there for what God is doing. In Holland, we heard from those who had escaped the massacre, that they would wait for him. But when he returned four years later, he discovered that no one had even

tried to work with the Nipsan in the interim.

When he got back to Irian, my father found out there had been a severe earthquake in the Nipsan area that had ruined all their gardens. The people were actually starving. So my dad sent MAF planes to fly over and drop sweet potatoes. But when the pilots checked back the next day they saw that the sweet potatoes were chopped up and thrown into the river. That's how hateful the people had become.

Then one day in 1978, Dad flew in with a helicopter and landed. He offered one of the men an axe which was accepted, meaning the missionary would be accepted again. We kept thinking it was a trap. But since that time, it has been truly amazing.

Before the massacre, it seemed everything was against us, even nature. Those first five years we were there, there was absolutely no fruit. Nothing. But since my father went back, young men are attending Bible school, and the Gospel is spreading so fast! People are so open to Christ! I remember the baptismal service that took place in Nipsan recently. The chief who led the massacre gave his testimony over the bull horn, the first one to get baptized. And the one who baptized him was none other than the Abanoho evangelist whose fourteen co-workers had been murdered! Imagine: Saboonwarek baptizes the chief who in turn will lead his people as missionaries to other tribes in the lowlands!

Are the primitive, animistic people groups of Indonesia resistant to the Gospel? If the Nipsan are any example, the answer is: Certainly not. They only needed a persistent presentation of God's loving character. Are the Muslim people groups of Indonesia resistant to the Gospel?

You pull off your headphones, lean forward and say, "Excuse me, Mr. Lubis. You mentioned there were no Christians on Bawean. Why is that?"

He folds the newspaper down and shakes his head. "I've seen your Christian America."

"You've been to the U.S.?"

"No," he says. "I watched your Christian America on television in London. I saw *Dallas* and *Falcon Crest*, and it simply would not work—that is, among my people."

You realize with goose bumps what his answer to your next question might mean in God's plan to reach every people—including the Baweans. So you stammer a little as you ask, "Has anyone ever explained to you what Christianity really is?"

Pono Lubis laboriously stretches his arm to check his watch. "We have fifteen minutes before my flight," he says. "I shall of course listen to what you have to say."

You lick your lips, breathe a prayer and think, "This is resistance?" Perched on the end of your suitcase, you launch into perhaps the most critical fifteen minutes of your life as you explain the whole counsel of the infinite heart of God.

So far we're fairly comfortable with the basic worldview that God is blessing His people in order to bless every people group on earth with His offer of redemption. His repeated promise to Abraham, Isaac and Jacob in Genesis is as clear as His unchangeable purpose.

But let's move on to the book of Exodus. Suddenly all our well-worn stories of baby Moses in the bulrushes, frogs and flies and rivers of blood, the parting of the Red Sea and the drowning of the Egyptians, the Ten Commandments and the wandering in the wilderness seem to suggest that God picked out the Hebrews and virtually dropped His interest in all the other heathen nations of the earth. We may have thought that the story of the Old Testament is simply an illustrative history of the antics and foibles of the Israelites as they formed a lineage to produce the Messiah.

But think again, remembering that God's purpose in blessing all the families of the earth is unchangeable. Let's take another glimpse at the stories of the Exodus in light of His heart for all peoples.

A Kingdom of Priests

Just before giving the Ten Commandments, God set Moses straight on Israel's role in His great purpose. Moses is to relay to the sons of Israel:

> If you will indeed obey My voice and keep My covenant, then you shall be My own possession among all the peoples, for all the earth is Mine; and you shall be to Me a kingdom of priests and a holy nation. (Exodus 19:5, 6)

The people were ecstatic about God's proposal and answered, "All that the Lord has spoken we will do!" (Exodus 19:8). And the rest of the chapter describes the "ordination service" the Lord performs to consecrate the Hebrews as "priests." But priests to minister in behalf of whom?

Aaron and his sons began the priestly ministry in behalf of the Children of Israel themselves; the entire tribe of the Levites then were given this responsibility as the nation grew. So the Israelites themselves were to mediate as priests for—the nations, of course!

Did they know what they were in for? Probably not. Representing God to all the people groups of the earth was quite a responsibility. They had no linguistic methodology for crossing cultural barriers, no transportation convenience, no completed Bible. But God promised that if they would simply obey Him, He would use them to bless every other people: "The people whom I formed for Myself, will declare My praise" (Isaiah 43:21).

He chose them, not to bless them at the exclusion of every other family of the earth, and not to single them out because of their superiority. Rather, He chose them to take on the responsibility of serving as priests whose parish was the entire world.

God promised that as they obeyed Him, the Children of Israel would be royal priests (one rendition of "kingdom of priests") blessed with two great privileges—God's personal protection and God's holiness: "You shall be My own possession . . . and you shall be . . . a holy nation" (Exodus 19:5, 6).

Israel was not originally a people; Abraham, you recall, was simply one of an Assyrian or barbarian people group. Out of His infinite grace, God formed Israel as His own people among all the other peoples. We will come to appreciate this fact as one of the most comforting truths we as New Testament believers enjoy as a people He has chosen to be His own possession.

God blessed Israel with His holiness. A holy nation or people indicates one "set apart for a particular service." God in His grace determined to set apart or sanctify this people that He formed not because of their inherent goodness, and not because of their superiority over other peoples: "The Lord did not set His love on you nor choose you because you were more in number than any of the peoples, for you were the fewest of all peoples, but because the Lord loved you and kept the oath which He swore to your forefathers" (Deuteronomy 7:7, 8). The King James Version of Exodus 19:5 refers to Israel as a people "above all the peoples." A better translation is "among all the peoples."

God's plan to bless this people and through their priestly intercession bless all the peoples of the earth would have worked wonderfully—if they had obeyed Him, keeping His covenant. Their prescribed part was simple, daily, devoted obedience. God promised His chosen people that "you will be called the priests of the Lord; you will be spoken of as ministers of our God" (Isaiah 61:6) with all the privileges of a priesthood. The results?

> Instead of humiliation [the "foreigners"] will shout for joy over their portion. Therefore they will possess a double portion in their land; everlasting joy will be theirs. . . . And I will make an everlasting covenant with them. Then their offspring will be known among the nations and their descendants in the midst of the peoples. All who see them will recognize them because they are the offspring whom the Lord has blessed. (Isaiah 61:7–9)

The nations, the people groups—not necessarily the political countries, remember—would be blessed as God's people represented Him in their protected, holy role as priests.

What would be their priestly message? A representation of God's character and reputation and saving grace. They were to uplift God's Name.

The Name Above All Names

A name in most cultures reveals the character of the one who carries the name; and God's name is no exception. Among the dozens of names given to God to describe His character, God chooses two for the Israelites to proclaim to the nations:

- *Elohim*, a plural term suggesting His triune, supreme deity—a name speaking of His power and role as Creator.
- *YHWH*, the self-existent One, the "I Am Who I Am" of Exodus 3:14. Used nearly 7,000 times in the Old Testament, this name is linked to God's holiness (Leviticus 11:44, 45), His hatred of sin (Genesis 6:3–7), and His provision of salvation (Isaiah 53:1, 5, 6, 10).

He uses these names as an expression of Who He is to Moses:

> The Lord, the Lord God, compassionate and gracious, slow to anger, and abounding in lovingkindness and truth; who keeps lov-

ingkindness for thousands, who forgives iniquity, transgression and sin; yet He will by no means leave the guilty unpunished, visiting the iniquity of fathers on the children and on the grandchildren to the third and fourth generations. (Exodus 34:6, 7)

Segments of this catechism-like description of God's character are repeated throughout the Old Testament (see Numbers 14:18; Psalm 68:15; 103:8; 145:8–21; Joel 2:13; Micah 7:18; Jonah 4:2; Malachi 1:11). This description and the meanings of *YHWH* were undoubtedly coupled with what the New Testament surprisingly calls "the Gospel [which was preached] beforehand to Abraham, saying, 'All the nations shall be blessed in you' " (Galatians 3:8). This "Old Testament Gospel" spoke of the coming One Who would crush Satan's head, by Whom "God would justify the Gentiles [all non-Jewish peoples] by faith" (Galatians 3:7).

The priestly Children of Israel were to proclaim the powerful, holy, redeeming character of the Lord God as they represented His Name:

Give thanks to the Lord, call on His name. Make known His deeds among the peoples; Make them remember that His name is exalted. Praise the Lord in song, for He has done excellent things; let this be known throughout the earth. (Isaiah 12:4, 5) (See also Psalm 48:10; 66:4; 86:8, 9; 96:1–10; 113:3, 4.)

The formula could work: God's kingdom of priests would obey, and God would ensure that through them His saving grace was proclaimed as a blessing to all peoples. The perfect scenario is seen by Jeremiah. God's people as His priests would say:

O Lord, my strength and my stronghold, and my refuge in the day of distress, to Thee the nations will come from the ends of the earth and say, "Our fathers have inherited nothing but falsehood, futility and no profit." Can man make gods for himself? Yet they are not gods!

"Therefore behold, I am going to make them know— . . . My power and My might; and they shall know that My name is [*YHWH*] the Lord." (Jeremiah 16:19–21)

The Message

Imagine the reaction of today's public to the interviews and incidents of the Exodus of the Children of Israel; focal in the news stories would be the reputation of the God of the Hebrews:

> Headline in the *Pyramid Pilot*: Hebrew Rebel Threatens Hail
> Next! The story: At daybreak Cairo time the renegade Hebrew
> Moses insisted on an audience with the Pharaoh. Apparently Phar-
> aoh had been sleepless through the night with boils—as reported
> throughout Egypt. This Moses was quoted as saying, "Thus says
> *YHWH*, the *Elohim* of the Hebrews . . . , 'This time I will send
> all My plagues on you . . . so that you may know that there is no
> one like Me in all the earth. . . . For this cause I have allowed you
> to remain, in order to show you My power and in order to proclaim
> My name through all the earth.' "
> What will it be this time? Blood, frogs, lice, flies, killing off
> the livestock, and boils—what else can this *YHWH-Elohim* hit us
> with to get the Pharaoh's attention? Rumor is that hail is the next
> stage in his promotional scheme.
> The trade routes are packed with foreigners fleeing from Egypt
> with the stories of these plagues. Estimates are that within three
> months every inn along the caravan roads from Europe to India,
> China to southern Africa will have heard of the humiliation of
> Pharaoh and the Egyptian gods. Many top cabinet posts are urging
> negotiations with Moses for fear of what this *YHWH* might devise
> as His next terrorist tactic. Unnamed sources said one of the Phar-
> aoh's servants has admitted "fearing the word of *Elohim*" and is
> currently bringing his servants and livestock in from the field. . . .

The news of this God-Who-is-not-to-be-toyed-with spread far and
wide throughout the events of the Exodus: God "divided the waters
before them to make for Himself an everlasting name. . . . So didst
Thou lead Thy people, to make for Thyself a glorious name" (Isaiah
63:12, 14).

God used His people regardless of their understanding of His purpose: "Our fathers in Egypt did not understand Thy wonders . . . but
rebelled by the sea, at the Red Sea. Nevertheless He saved them for the
sake of His name, that He might make His power known" (Psalm 106:7,
8).

The eminence of His name was the leverage Moses used to "convince" God not to destroy the golden-calf-worshiping Israelites: "Why
should the Egyptians speak, saying, 'With evil intent He brought them
out to kill them in the mountains and to destroy them from the face of
the earth'?" (Exodus 32:12). If God had brought the Israelites through

such miraculous events only to blast them into oblivion in the desert, who would want to follow Him? Imagine the Egyptians who responded in reverential fear to the God of the Hebrews, whom they learned was compassionate and gracious, yet would not leave the guilty unpunished who suddenly reverted to the gods of Egypt. These old familiar gods might have been humiliated by this *YHWH-Elohim*, but at least they didn't trick their followers into following them into annihilation!

It's one of the basic themes of the Old Testament's stories of settling into the Promised Land: The name of the Lord is to be acknowledged by all peoples. When the wilderness-wandering generation of mumblers had died off, the new generation of the Children of Israel crossed over the Jordan River on dry ground. Joshua later explained to the people, "The Lord your God dried up the waters of the Jordan before you . . . that all the peoples of the earth may know that the hand of the Lord is mighty" (Joshua 4:23, 24).

In Jericho, the prostitute Rahab explains why she has protected the Israelite spies:

> For we have heard how the Lord [*YHWH*, the holy Redeemer] dried up the water of the Red Sea before you when you came out of Egypt, and what you did to the two kings of the Amorites. . . . And when we heard it, our hearts melted and no courage remained in any man any longer because of you; for the Lord [*YHWH*] your God [*Elohim*, the strong Creator], He is God in heaven above and on earth beneath." (Joshua 2:10, 11)

Rahab's knowledge of Who God is came only through traders' stories of the experiences of the Israelites; and yet from this revelation of His name, she believed, obeyed and was justified (Hebrews 1:31; James 2:25).

When the men of Ai first defeated the sons of Israel, Joshua complained, "O Lord, what can I say since Israel has turned their back before their enemies? For the Canaanites and all the inhabitants of the land will hear of it. . . . And what wilt Thou do for Thy great name?" (Joshua 7:8, 9).

Envoys from the Gibeonites told Joshua, "Your servants have come from a very far country because of the fame of the Lord your God; for we have heard the report of Him and all that He did in Egypt" (Joshua 9:9).

God's Unchangeable Purpose

Why did God perform incredible miracles to free Israel from slavery in Egypt and lead them through the wilderness to a land flowing with milk and honey?

Our usual answer has something to do with their being His *chosen* people. But chosen for what? Chosen to be blessed, while all the other people groups of the world suffer, captives to Satan's dominion of darkness? Chosen and specially treated, like spoiled children, their disobediences tolerated until they finally produce a Messiah? Or chosen as a kingdom of priests to perform the responsibilities of God's purpose—to offer redemptive blessing to all the peoples of the earth? To be used as set-apart vessels to demonstrate God's character, His name, to all the nations?

Spend some time rethinking many of your favorite stories from Exodus, Numbers, Joshua and Judges. How did God use each incident to further His eternal, unchangeable purpose to bless His people and through them bless every people?

Closer to Home

Let's back up a bit and bring this chapter's input a little closer to home.

Why has God chosen *me*? Why has He left me on the earth, instead of whisking me off to the joyous ease of heaven the instant I received Christ? To live a blessed life while millions from unreached people groups suffer, captives of Satan's dominion of darkness? To be specially treated like a spoiled child, my disobediences tolerated until I finally die to live in Christlikeness eternally? Or have I been chosen as one in a kingdom of priests to perform the responsibilities of God's purpose—to offer redemptive blessing to all the peoples of the earth? To be used as a set-apart vessel to demonstrate God's character, His name, to all the nations?

What if I were to spend some quality time rethinking some of my favorite experiences? How can God use an incident I went through to further His eternal, unchangeable purpose—to bless me as one of His people and through me bless every people?

The parallel here isn't simply the author's application. It's biblical according to the New Testament. If you are a believer, you are one of "a chosen race, a royal priesthood, a holy nation, a people for God's own possession" (1 Peter 2:9). Why?

The verse continues: "That you may proclaim the excellencies of Him who has called you out of darkness into His marvelous light."

Think of it. You're not foremost a Jew or gentile—Germanic or Arabic or Korean or Kurdish or Slavic or Han Chinese. You're foremost a member of the people group of God: "You once were not a people, but now you are the people of God!" (1 Peter 2:10). We believers are priests (Revelation 1:6) not for our own benefit, but for the nations. You are a priest to the people groups of the earth.

*B*efore you walk out into the hot jetwash from the Jakarta airport to get on the Air India plane for Calcutta, you pray once more for Pono Lubis and his Bawean people. And you realize with a start that you've just performed one of the basic functions of a priest: You've ministered in intercessory prayer for the Baweans, one of the remaining 12,000 people groups of the earth.

For Further Thought

1. Study and meditate on 1 Peter 2:9, 10 to clarify your personal and your church's standing as a *kingdom of priests*.
2. Find a map of Indonesia that shows the island of Bawean north of Java and Irian Jaya. Check out anthropological, travel, and history books on Indonesia. Jot notes to more clearly pray that the Baweans might be reached with the Gospel and the Nipsan might be further equipped to be missionaries to neighboring unreached people groups.
3. Pray daily during the coming month for direction on how you can be a holy and effective "priest" on behalf of the Bawean people.
4. Once you've done some homework on a people—whether the Uzbeks, Naxi, Japanese, Hmong, Meo, Baweans or Nipsan—share your insights with at least one friend this week.

C H A P T E R 6

Ups and Downs:
The Best of Times,
The Worst of Times

*C*alcutta. After a week in the city, you are desensitized a bit to the swirl of smells and sights of poverty, the 12 million people around you, the half million who live on the streets. You're bouncing along on a city bus trying to finish a dog-eared paperback about Ghandi, and you're still upset from an early entry in the biography. When Ghandi was asked about the authenticity of the Gospel, he replied that he rejected Christianity because of what he saw—and didn't see—in the character of Christians.

But what if Hindus could see the character of *Elohim*, the Deity of power—of *YHWH*, the God who is a personal Redeemer, a holy Savior! You remember a recent survey report you read: 25% of the Hindus in India would consider becoming a Christian if they could do it without losing their cultural and family ties, without becoming, in effect, a Westerner.

You rest the biography in your lap and wearily gaze blankly out the dusty bus window at the milling crowds along a main street lined with sophisticated office buildings. There's an old blind beggar being whisked away from the doors of the opulent Oberoi Grand Hotel. You hear the constant clanging of cymbals as sacrifices are made to Kali, Calcutta's namesake, the goddess of death and destruction. But she is, after all, only one of the 33 million gods worshiped in India.

You remember the tales of Ghasi Das and the remarkable Satnamis, worshipers of the true God. (In Hindi, "true" is *sat* and "name" is *nam*. Thus *Satnamis* for the Christian.)

It was 1817. "Throw out your idols! Worship only the true

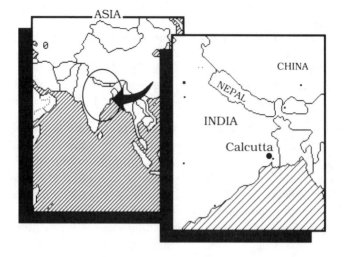

God! Quit eating meat—it lowers you in the eyes of all Hindus. Dress in white. Live simply. Wait for the coming of a red-faced man with a big hat on his head and a big book in his hand. Do what he tells you!"

This was the message the peasant Ghasi Das shouted across the flat fields of the great plain in the southeast corner of Madhya Pradesh. Of the low-caste Chamar people, Ghasi Das walked nearly 400 miles east on a pilgrimage to this very city—Calcutta. At the holy Ganges River, Ghasi Das followed the riverbank to the mouth where he came upon a red-faced man with a big hat on his head and a huge book. William Carey, the "father of modern missions," was preaching on God's heart for the peoples of India. Carey had initiated the first mission agency when the leadership of his church told him, "Young man, if God wants to evangelize the heathen, He can certainly do it without our help!"

But God was now doing it with William Carey's "help." And Ghasi Das listened intently to this foreigner's twisted Hindi.

Ghasi immediately set out with his message for the Chamars: "Throw out your idols! Worship the true God!" It was a call to become a new people with a new, true God; and the message found immediate widespread acceptance.

The Chamars asked, "What is the name of the true God whom you proclaim?"

"I don't know," the peasant replied, "but His name is the true name."

The Satnamis tossed out their idols and waited for the red-faced man with the big book to tell them more.

The red-faced man never came. But other foreigners did—foreigners who virtually told the True-Namers that if they would become Westernized, they could grow in worshiping the true God.

You suddenly realize you're nodding off in the Calcutta bus. You slap yourself awake, look at the faces on the sidewalks in the dusty sunlight. And you're suddenly glad you don't know everything; you're glad you're not God. Imagine knowing the hearts of every one of these millions giving themselves to the domain of the goddess of death, of the billions worldwide. Imagine knowing the despair of those seeking the True Name, of those disappointed by some of the missionaries of the past whose idea of blessing the nations was converting them to Western culture. Imagine the heart of God breaking for the 55,000 who die daily without ever hearing the True Name.

For the first time in your around-the-world journey, you slump, breathless in your seat, and you weep.

The Ups and Downs

Moses made God's covenant perfectly clear to the sons of Israel: "If you will diligently obey the Lord your God . . . all the peoples of the earth shall see that you are called by the name of the Lord . . . and the Lord will make you abound" (Deuteronomy 28:1–11).

Before Joshua died at the ripe old age of 110, he reminded Israel to serve the Lord and to consider the dire consequences of disobedience. The Chosen People's response? "Far be it from us that we should forsake the Lord to serve other gods; for the Lord our God is He who . . . preserved us . . . among all the peoples through whose midst we passed" (Joshua 24:16, 17).

But we all know the story: God soon had to reprimand the sons of Israel with "You have not obeyed Me" (Judges 2:2). They refused to drive out the inhabitants of the Promised Land; instead they intermarried and began to worship other gods.

Incidentally, why did God give such drastic orders as: "You shall not leave alive anything that breathes. But you shall utterly destroy them. . . ." (Deuteronomy 20:16, 17)? Because God knew their "detestable things which they have done for their gods" (sexually focused religious practices) would infect and destroy the Israelites as a people. The modern-day AIDS epidemic across the continent of Africa threatens the very existence of whole people groups. Israel would have undergone pestilence, consumption, fever, inflammation, boils, tumors, scabs and itch from which they could not be healed—madness, blindness, bewilderment of heart—until they were destroyed because they would not obey the Lord (Deuteronomy 28:19–45).

Second, God allowed the total destruction of people groups such as the Hittites, Amorites, Perizzites, Hivites, Jebusites and Canaanites because He knew they would never as a people turn to Him. That is, the Hittites as a people would never repent even though some individual Hittites such as Uriah (2 Samuel 11) would respond to stand before the throne of the Lamb (Revelation 5:9). God in His infinite wisdom knows when the final judgment of a people group is inevitable, when they will experience nothing but the disease, the suffering, the futility of their bondage of darkness. Make no mistake, the fearsome God of the Old Testament and the God of the twenty-first century does allow the destruction of people who refuse to respond to the light He has given them—whether it is the initial light of creation, conscience and instinct or the further light of the Gospel as revealed in Scripture. (See Psalm 19:1–4; 65:8; Romans 1:18–23.)

Because of the Israelites' disobedience, the death of Joshua was followed by nearly 400 years of roller-coaster ups and downs as God's kingdom of priests discredited His name—then repented under a God-appointed leader—then discredited God's name—then repented under a God-appointed leader—then. . . . (See Samuel's recap of these events in 1 Samuel 12:8–12.)

The Ups

Three—and only three—kings ruled a united Israel: Saul, David and Solomon. Samuel appointed Saul as the first king even while scolding the nation for their rejection of the Lord God as their king: "Your wickedness is great which you have done in the sight of the Lord by asking for yourselves a king" (1 Samuel 12:17). But Samuel also warned them not to turn aside from following the Lord, "for the Lord will not abandon His people on account of His great name" (12:22). Yet Saul proved unworthy to lead a nation whose God was the Lord.

David's exploits in the name of the Lord are some of the most familiar stories of the Old Testament. He shouted to the Philistine Goliath, "You come to me with a sword, a spear, and a javelin, but I come to you in the name of the Lord of hosts, the God of the armies of Israel, whom you have taunted. This day the Lord will deliver you up into my hands . . . that all the earth may know that there is a God in Israel" (1 Samuel 17:45, 46).

And David is probably the one who penned or commissioned such verses as "God blesses us, that all the ends of the earth may fear Him" (Psalm 67:7). The faithful Israelites of David's time sang that line over and over again. Perhaps David's constant reference in his psalms to "the peoples," "the nations" and "the ends of the earth" suggest why he became "a man after God's own heart"—the heart that yearns after the world's lost.

And Israel's role as a shining light to all the peoples of the earth was probably never as prominent as during the early reign of David's son Solomon. The Israelite of Solomon's glory days would say, "Of course, God blesses us to be a blessing to the nations." Hadn't they all been at the temple dedication ceremonies and memorized Solomon's dedicatory prayer?

> Concerning the foreigner who . . . comes from a far country for Thy name's sake (for they will hear of Thy great name and Thy mighty hand, and of Thine outstretched arm); when he comes and prays toward this house, hear Thou in heaven . . . and do according to all for which the foreigner calls to Thee, in order that all the peoples of the earth may know Thy name, to fear Thee, as do Thy people Israel, and that they may know that this house which I have built is called by Thy name. (1 Kings 8:41–43)

Every time the Israelites came into the silver-decked and gold-covered temple consecrated by the very heart of God (1 Kings 9:3), they entered through what became known in later days as "The Court of the Gentiles." In the days of Isaiah, God confirmed the international scope of His blessing on this temple: "Also the foreigners who join themselves to the Lord . . . I will bring to My holy mountain, and make them joyful in My house of prayer. . . . For My house will be called a house of prayer for all the peoples" (Isaiah 56:6, 7). (Is it any wonder Jesus drove out the moneychangers and peddlers from the Court of the Gentiles, shouting this reference? See Mark 11:15–17.)

Even those from the outlying countryside of Israel were reminded that Israel's blessing had to do with the uplifting of God's name among the nations when the Queen of Sheba came to town. The trade routes from China to India to southern Africa to Spain buzzed with the news: This ruler of the Sabeans in the southern region of Arabia traveled on camelback for 1,200 miles to meet Solomon. She brought him about $50,000 in gold, and "a very great amount of spices and precious stones."

The obvious question was asked and answered all along the routes: Why did she come? Because "when the queen of Sheba heard about the fame of Solomon concerning the name of the Lord, she came to test him with difficult questions" (1 Kings 10:1). The name of the Lord— the personal Redeemer, the holy, eternal One, the all-powerful Creator—the God of Solomon provoked her quest.

Apparently Solomon answered all her "difficult questions" concerning the name of the Lord and His blessing. "It was a true report," she said, "which I heard in my own land. . . . How blessed are your men, how blessed are these your servants. . . . Blessed be the Lord your God" (1 Kings 10:6–9).

God was accomplishing His unchangeable purpose of blessing His people to be a blessing to all peoples. Then Solomon fell in love.

The Downs

Imagine. Solomon marries the daughter of the pharaoh of Egypt. He marries a Moabitess and an Ammonite. He marries an Edomite woman, a Sidonian and a Hittite woman. And another Hittite woman. And another. Can you imagine 700 wedding ceremonies? And keeping track of 300 mistresses?

Obviously the potential for Solomon's marital problems was great; he loved and married a few too many hundreds of women. And the potential for spiritual danger increased with each new wife. God had expressly commanded not to intermarry with other peoples because "they will surely turn your heart away after their gods" (Deuteronomy 7:3, 4, and 1 Kings 11:2).

And that is exactly what happened. As Solomon gave in to the pleading of his wives to be able to worship their own gods, his own "heart was not wholly devoted to the Lord his God, as the heart of David his father had been. For Solomon went after Ashtoreth the goddess of the Sidonians and after Milcom the detestable idol of the Ammonites. . . . Then Solomon built a high place for Chemosh the detestable idol of Moab, on the mountain which is east of Jerusalem, and for Molech the detestable idol of the sons of Ammon. Thus also he did for all his foreign wives, who burned incense and sacrificed to their gods" (1 Kings 11:4–8).

More is at stake here, of course, than Solomon's spiritual welfare. Even more is on the line than his poor performance as a role model for his own people. The name of the Lord is being blasphemed. And the news spreads quickly.

Solomon has a household-full of seven hundred "foreign correspondents" who pass news regularly on to their royal families, their friends, their own people groups. Imagine Solomon's wives listening for their homeland dialects in the marketplace, catching up on home-front news from travelers and traders coming through Jerusalem, the world trade-route center.

And what news do they pass on? Great news for the homeland! "Solomon is now worshiping our god! Our gods are back in vogue!" And as the traders caravan out of Jerusalem, the news is validated. High on the mountain east of Jerusalem are temples to Milcom, Molech, Ashtoreth and other gods.

God's reputation is being destroyed.

The Never-Ending Story

A thousand years later the apostle Paul complained to the Jews that "the name of God is blasphemed among [the peoples] because of you" (Romans 2:24). See also Isaiah 52:5.

A thousand years after that the marauding Crusaders slaughtered the "infidel" Muslim men, women and children of the Mediterranean in the name of Christ, and Islam has never forgotten the atrocities of these "Christians."

Nearly a thousand years after the Crusades, Mahatma Ghandi in India says he rejects Christ's Gospel because of the demeanor of those who call themselves His people.

And in Emakhandeni, Zimbabwe, a husky man dips a wad of snuff, a ritual of ancestral spirit worship, and tells his two young Christian visitors, "This Jesus and this Bible is from white men to cool down Africans so whites can rule over them and tax them and steal their land.

You young people swallow many things without chewing them. This Jesus is the ancestral spirit for whites, but we Africans have nothing to do with Him. We have our own ancestors."

Frank Mayis and Lifa Ndlovu, on one of their first evangelistic visits, aren't quite sure how to respond. "Do you pray to God?" Lifa asks.

"You're too young to know anything!" the big old man says. "I can't pray to God directly. He's too great. I have to speak to the spirits of my ancestors and ask them to speak to God for me because they're closer to Him. God is too great! This Jesus is just a white man!"

Now thousands of miles northeast of Zimbabwe, across the Indian Ocean, you step down from the bus and trip over chunks of broken concrete in the debris of the Calcutta street. And you wonder how you've been doing as a priest, a representative of the character of God.

You round a corner to a dirt lane of sour-smelling market stalls and weave through milling shoppers in dusty white. You pass under strands of flax and tapestries; flies persistently cling to your shirt. Within the block you count four video stalls—booths with a television and video-cassette recorder playing to audiences of two or three. You hear the familiar musical theme of the old *Bonanza* cowboy series of the 60's and 70's. You slump against a post and watch a corner of the screen at one stall showing *Dynasty*. Another is blaring the saxaphoned score to an old *Mike Hammer* episode.

Store after store offers American cigarettes and glamor magazines. And you glimpse in several dark, back-row stalls the brassy colors of porno magazines from the West. You feel the almost palpable darkness of Satanic oppression over this city like a net over your shoulders.

And you find yourself getting angry. Because you know that imperialism, materialism and sexual obsession is what much of the spiritually blinded, unreached world thinks of as "Christian." Because of the reputation of "Christian" Europe and North America, the name of God is often blasphemed among the world's peoples.

You know that any nation that claims to be God's people and that discredits His name is in for trouble. "Taking God's name in vain" doesn't mean swearing so much as dragging His character—His Deity, power, redemption and holiness—through the mud. And the realization scares you. As you slip into a Western-style travel office to book passage on a coal ship to Djibouti, you remember a dire ranting from the prophet Ezekiel:

76

I chose Israel . . . to bring them out of Egypt into a land that I had selected for them . . . but they rebelled against Me. Then I resolved to pour out my wrath on them . . . but I acted for the sake of My name, that it should not be profaned in the sight of the nations. . . .

And I gave them My statutes . . . but the house of Israel rebelled against Me in the wilderness. . . . Then I resolved to pour out My wrath on them . . . but I acted for the sake of My name, that it should not be profaned in the sight of the nations. . . .

And I said to their children in the wilderness, "Do not walk in the statutes of your fathers. . . ." But the children rebelled against Me. . . . So I resolved to pour out My wrath on them. . . . But I withdrew My hand and acted for the sake of My name, that it should not be profaned in the sight of the nations. (Ezekiel 20:5–22)

The ups and downs are obvious. Mostly the downs. Israel was fast becoming like any other people group: "We will be like the nations, like the tribes of the lands, serving wood and stone" (Ezekiel 20:32). But God would persevere in His great plan to reach every people. In spite of their evil intentions, He says, "I shall prove Myself holy among you in the sight of the nations . . . Then you will know that I am the Lord when I have dealt with you for My name's sake" (Ezekiel 20:41, 44).

*T*oday, God's reputation among the peoples of the earth is at stake every time His people go after other "gods." Every time they blaspheme His name among the nations. The Old Testament warnings that God resolves to pour out His wrath makes you uncomfortable. And for the first time in days, you think about home—the country with the motto, "In God We Trust."

For Further Thought

1. Read through Isaiah 56:6, 7 and Mark 11:15–17. When was the last time you heard a message on the fact that Jesus' indignation in this very familiar New Testament story was at least in part due to Israel's selfishness in not allowing the gentiles—the "nations"—to worship at the temple? What does this suggest about our own selfishness in concentrating so much on top-line interpretations of Scripture that we rarely mention the bottom line of God's heart for every people group?

2. Get out your world map or globe and pinpoint some of the geographical areas we've covered in this part of our global journey: Calcutta, Jerusalem, "Sheba" or southern Arabia, Zimbabwe. How is the reputation of the Lord—His name that speaks of deity and personal redemption—treated in these locations today?

3. Pray for the dozens of various people groups clustered in Calcutta. The futility of trying to feed every malnourished street orphan or of teaching job skills to every homeless youth can keep us from praying realistically at all about such depressing situations and groups of humanity. But aren't we angry at such injustice—that Satan keeps these hundreds of thousands captive in his evil domain?

Our anger alone can keep us crying out to God for Calcutta. He promises that "blessed is the people group whose God is the Lord." If we pray against the strongholds of Satan over this city, if we petition God to thrust forth hundreds of church-planting teams into Calcutta, as people group after people group make the Lord their God, Satan's control will be broken. Jesus Christ says to the hopeless, desperate people of the world's mega-cities that He has come "to preach the Gospel to the poor . . . to proclaim release to the captives, and recovery of sight to the blind, to set free those who are downtrodden, to proclaim the favorable year of the Lord" (Luke 4:18, 19). The babies and young people and the aged of Calcutta will have a chance to enjoy the blessing of God! Pray for Calcutta.

4. Review the information in Chapter 2 regarding the interlink of the spiritual and natural worlds. Jot down some of the details you've learned in this chapter about Calcutta, and share your concerns for serious prayer for that great city with several friends.

CHAPTER 7

Purses With Holes: Fitting Into God's Purpose—The Hard Way

Y ou're cool and comfortable in the fore stateroom of a sparkling-white coal freighter southbound through the Seychelles off the coast of Africa. The Indian Ocean is an unearthly indigo blue under the bright sun. You pull out a pamphlet you've kept in your reading bag: *The Most Christian Nation on Earth*. Resting up for your upcoming safari into the bush of Malawi, you sprawl back on your bunk and read:

The United States is known around the world as a "Christian" nation. Let's look at the facts as of 1991:
- 1,485 Christian radio stations
- 300 Christian television programs
- 96% "believers in God"
- 148 million professing Christians
- 62% say they have "made a commitment to Jesus Christ that is still important in their life today"
- 70 million born-again believers

Christianity is part of the American culture. Recently, a woman in Texas thanks the Lord on a nationwide secular television station that she was preserved from a tornado that struck her town. A quiz show host asks contestants for an example of a "life-changing experience." Without hesitation someone answers, "Accepting Jesus Christ as Lord and Savior." Gospel music concerts are being sponsored by big businesses such as McDonald's. *Time* carries an extensive interview with evangelist Billy Graham. In 1990 Secretary of State James Baker gives a ringing testimony at the Presidential Prayer Breakfast. Supermarkets and drugstores carry Christian plaques with the Lord's Prayer and the Ten Commandments on them. Bibles and other Christian books adorn their shelves. There are more "fish" on cars than in the supermarkets.

The Pilgrim fathers' reason for establishing the country was "for the glory of God and the founding of the Christian faith." The Declaration of Independence states that "all men are endowed by God with certain inalienable rights." Fifty of the 55 men who instituted the U.S. Constitution were professing Christians. We have "In God We Trust" on our currency, and our favorite national hymn proclaims that God's grace is shed upon us. Justices of Peace in most states officiate using legal marriage vows that speak of the "sanctity of marriage in the Lord Jesus Christ."

The Bible says that righteousness exalts a nation, that its health will "spring forth because of righteousness." God will honor a culture that will honor Him. And if America is as godly as she seems, it will be reflected in her land, right? Let's look at some more facts:

- Ten million Americans have been diagnosed with serious, long-term mental illness. Since state institutions can house only 119,000 patients, many of the rest roam the streets of big cities.
- There are an estimated three million homeless; 52% of these are within families.
- One million teenagers run away from home each year; some of these become one of the thousands of suicides (38,000 each year in California alone).
- The national debt is over $152,000,000,000,000.
- The headlines speak of recession, government paralysis and war.
- In only four months one year, 500,000 jobs were lost in once-stable corporations.
- Billions of dollars were lost through the collapse of Savings & Loans failures.
- In one year Americans spent $240 billion on gambling.
- In that same year 2.5 million abused, missing and abducted children were reported. Reports show that the number-one killers of children are their own parents.
- Each year, 5,000 women are killed by domestic violence; 23,000 are murdered annually. Drunk drivers kill 25,000 people yearly.
- Grisly satanic murders and mass killings are commonplace. Drive-by shootings and other gang- and drug-related murders

are beyond police control in many cities. Violence and drug usage have so infiltrated the public school system that over 500,000 children are educated at home by their parents.

- Fifty thousand drug-addicted children are born each year in California alone.
- Every year 800,000 babies are born to unwed teenagers.
- An additional one million babies are aborted each year—146,000 of these abortions are done in the seven-nine month period!

Marriages breaking apart, wide-spread alcoholism, epidemic drug problems, overt racism, massive financial pressures in the home and in commerce, to say nothing of the natural disasters like tornadoes, hurricanes, floods, earthquakes, and droughts—it's hard to equate it all with God blessing this nation!

"Well," you might say, "that is all outside of the church." Is it? A recent survey on university campuses uncovered that nearly half of those who called themselves "evangelicals" thought that premarital sex was okay. In fact, a confidential study done by *Christianity Today* among pastors showed that nearly one in four had been involved in some sort of sexual sin.

Satan understood the principle of inoculation long before man discovered it. His great victory in the twentieth century has been to convince the Church to fling open its doors and tell unregenerate America to simply "ask Jesus into your heart." The modern Gospel is often void of reference to sin, law, obedience, righteousness, holiness, repentance and hell. . . .[1]

There's more, but you don't want to read it. You throw the pamphlet down and trudge across the cool metal floor of your coal ship stateroom. You stare out through an open porthole and get a breath of humid seabreeze. Frankly, you just don't like to think about the possibility of God removing His blessing from the American culture. You can't wait to get home—home to clean, even streets, plenty of fresh food in sparkling grocery stores, Kentucky Fried Chicken take-outs. You want to be home for high school football games and *The Cosby Show* and logical people and apple pie. What is God saying to America in the rush of the quickening pace as He completes His historic, unchangeable plan?

The warnings your American culture has endured about sliding into moral depravity, doing drugs, ignoring church affiliation, all seem—

---

[1]Adapted from the pamphlet by Ray Comfort, Living Waters Publications, Bellflower, CA.

admit it—exaggerated and therefore a bit ineffective. After all, there are and have been plenty of worse cultures. Even from what you've learned in your global journey so far, more blatantly evil activity has gone on for centuries in all sorts of long-standing cultures. You stare out at the sea and think about the decency and good-will of America— misunderstood, maligned as she is worldwide, America still tries to be a good, compassionate people. Doesn't she?

Is America so pervasively evil that she's headed for hell? Of course you can find evil here and there among her people. But when you've staggered through the atmosphere of evil in cities like Calcutta, when you've walked in the spiritual oppression of Osaka like a dreamer who can't run when danger is imminent, the worst of San Francisco seems like a Sunday school picnic. Besides, America's older generation has always complained that the younger generation is disgustingly loose, uneducated, off-track and going to the dogs. Is America really in trouble because of all the sins she commits?

Or does judgment loom because of what she omits?

"To whom much is given, much is required." And despite many characteristics to the contrary, America was founded to be a "Christian nation." Is her basic crime as a people that she's gone after other gods that demand that she hoard God's blessings rather than extend them to all peoples? If that's the case, no amount of repentance of America's Christians to clean up unrighteousness will fully heal the land until that repentance includes a recommitment to be God's priests to the nations, the remaining unreached people groups.

The parallels to Scripture are obvious.

For the Sake of His Name

In the Old Testament, God's people knew they were to "say among the nations, 'The Lord reigns' " (Psalm 96:10). In the most effective teaching method of the day, their memorized songs, they sang:

Oh give thanks to the Lord, call upon His name;
Make known His deeds among the peoples. . . .
Sing to the Lord, all the earth;
Proclaim good tidings of His salvation from day to day;
Tell of His glory among the nations,
His wonderful deeds among all the peoples. . . .
Ascribe to the Lord, O families of the peoples,

Ascribe to the Lord glory and strength,
Ascribe to the Lord the glory due His name;
Bring an offering, and come before Him;
Worship the Lord in holy array. . . .
Let the heavens be glad, and let the earth rejoice;
And let them say among the nations,
"The Lord reigns!" (1 Chronicles 16:8, 23, 24, 28, 29, 31)

But about 250 years after David wrote this song, Israel's ups and downs finally resulted in judgment.

Warnings of the Prophets

Jonah, Hosea and Amos were God's spokesmen to the ten northern tribes of Israel. Jonah's message wasn't simply a story of the importance of personal obedience. His experience was the story of Israel's refusal to bless all the peoples of the earth—especially her enemies! Nineveh was the nerve center of the Assyrian dynasty, Israel's worst enemy and probably one of the most ruthless and savage people groups of all time. Jonah—Israel—didn't like the idea that God would ask such irritating questions as, "Should I not have compassion on Nineveh?" (Jonah 4:11).

Jonah evidenced Israel's attitude toward blessing disdained peoples when he pouted at God's salvation of the Assyrian city: Nineveh's repentance "greatly displeased Jonah, and he became very angry . . . and said, 'Please, Lord, was not this what I said while I was still in my own country? Therefore, in order to forestall this [salvation of Nineveh] I fled to Tarshish, for I knew that Thou art a gracious and compassionate God, slow to anger and abundant in lovingkindness and one who relents concerning calamity' " (Jonah 4:1, 2). Jonah and Israel knew that all nations would respond to the message they had of God's character. But they refused to proclaim Him. They would have to learn the hard way that you don't fool with the purpose of the God of the universe.

Hosea's experience of loving a faithless wife likewise was a painful one-man-play that acted out the ten northern tribes' impending judgment. Hosea's message warned that unfaithfulness to God not only goes against the grain of His purpose; it also breaks His heart. Israel refused to be God's priests for the nations—sometimes obstinately, sometimes ignorantly: "My people are destroyed for lack of knowledge. Because you have rejected knowledge, I also will reject you from being My priest" (Hosea 4:6).

As Israel lost its sense of purpose as a kingdom of priests, it lost its distinction as a holy, set-apart people: "Israel is swallowed up; they are now among the nations like a vessel in which no one delights" (Hosea 8:8). God showered them with blessings that they were to enjoy and to pass on in His name to all peoples. But they squandered all His blessings on the pursuit of their own gods: "Israel . . . produces fruit for himself. The more his fruit, the more altars he made; the richer his land, the better he made the sacred pillars" (Hosea 10:1).

God's call to Israel through Hosea was a warning of compassion. God would accomplish His purpose regardless of Israel's compliance. But why do it the hard way knowing it would bring pain to God's people and pain to the very heart of God? "My heart is turned over within Me," God said. "All My compassions are kindled" (Hosea 11:8). And He insisted there was still time to repent and return to voluntarily represent His name: "The Lord, the God of hosts; the Lord is His name. Therefore, return to your God. Observe kindness and justice, and wait for your God continually" (Hosea 12:5, 6). Israel needed desperately to "return" in repentance, clean up her sins and once again become the holy nation that could proclaim God's character of kindness and justice.

But out of stubbornness or ignorance, they would not return.

Amos explained his fellow prophets' dismal warnings with, "Surely the Lord God does nothing unless He reveals His secret counsel to His servants the prophets" (Amos 3:7). These irritating prophets kept spoiling the people's good time with negative comments such as, "Woe to those who are at ease in Zion, and to those who feel secure . . . who recline on beds of ivory and sprawl on their couches . . . and eat lambs from the flock . . . who drink wine from sacrificial bowls" (Amos 6:1–6). God has a larger purpose than the comfort of His people.

In the southern kingdom of Judah, God's red-alert of judgment came through Micah, whose name means "Who is like *YHWH*?" Micah warned that, when you are called by God's name, you don't challenge *Elohim- YHWH*: "Hear, O peoples, all of you; Listen, O earth and all it contains . . . the Lord is coming forth from His place. . . . The mountains will melt under Him. . . . All this is for the rebellion of

Jacob" (Micah 1:2–5). About 150 years later, Judah began to fulfill God's unchangeable purpose—the hard way.

And accomplishing God's purpose the hard way was not going to be easy. God promised to His people that, in order to show His character as a God of holiness as well as compassion, "One third of you will die by plague or be consumed by famine among you, one third will fall by the sword around you, and one third I will scatter to every wind. . . . Moreover, I will make you a desolation and a reproach among the nations. . . . So it will be . . . a warning . . . to the nations who surround you" (Ezekiel 5:12–15). With 95% of the world's trading routes passing through Israel, the nations of the earth would soon learn that you don't doublecross the God of Israel.

The prophet Ezekiel clearly spelled out God's rationale:

> Thus says the LORD God, "It is not for your sake, O house of Israel, that I am about to act, but for My holy name which you have profaned among the nations where you went. And I will vindicate the holiness of My great name . . . which you have profaned in their midst. Then the nations will know that I am the Lord," declares the Lord God, "when I prove Myself holy among you in their sight." (Ezekiel 36:22, 23; see also Ezekiel 39:21–23.)

After the pain of the captivity, God himself explained that since His people "refused to pay attention and turned a stubborn shoulder and stopped their ears from hearing, and they made their hearts like flint . . . I scattered them with a storm wind among all the nations whom they have not known" (Zechariah 7:11, 12, 14).

God's Ongoing Twofold Program

Even when Israel refused to be a blessing to the nations, God carried on His predestined program. He would use even these painful events of judgment to announce: "Turn to Me and be saved, all the ends of the earth; for I am God, and there is no other. I have sworn by Myself, the word has gone forth from My mouth . . . and will not turn back. . . . My purpose will be established, and I will accomplish all My good pleasure. . . . Truly I have spoken; truly I will bring it to pass. I have planned it, surely I will do it" (Isaiah 45:22, 23; 46:10, 11).

Even as God's people underwent judgment, the purposeful God of compassion promised that their role as His chosen people, as a light to the world's peoples or gentiles (Isaiah 60:1–3) would continue and be focused in the coming Servant (Isaiah 49:6).

God said, "Pay attention to Me, O My people; and give ear to Me, O My nation; for a law will go forth from Me, and I will set My justice for a light of the peoples. . . . The coastlands will wait for Me. . . . When the Lord restores Zion . . . the Lord has bared His holy arm in the sight of all the nations, that all the ends of the earth may see the salvation of our God" (Isaiah 51:4, 5; 52:8–10). God's unchangeable purpose would continue through His people.

In captivity in Babylon, individuals who were called by God's name carried on their roles proclaiming the excellencies of His name. Daniel's witness to the character of God resulted in emperor Nebuchadnezzar's testimony to God's greatness (Daniel 4) and Darius' incredible proclamation "to all the peoples, nations, and men of every language who were living in all the land . . . I make a decree that in all the dominion of my kingdom men are to fear and tremble before the God of Daniel; for He is the living God and enduring forever . . . He delivers and rescues . . ." (Daniel 6:25–27).

At the close of the 70 years of captivity, God blessed His people again. The Persian ruler Cyrus acknowledged "the Lord, the God of heaven" and allowed about 50,000 Jews to return to their land laden with "silver and gold, with goods and cattle, together with a freewill offering for the house of God which is in Jerusalem" (Ezra 1:2–4).

What did God's people do with these blessings? Almost 15 years after they arrived back in the land, they still had done nothing about rebuilding God's house of prayer for the nations. They had used some of the proceeds of Cyrus' generosity to buy cedar wood from Lebanon. But instead of using it to build up God's house, they installed the new cedar paneling in their own homes! God sent the prophet Haggai to slap them awake: Did His people really want another round of judgment?

Scripture often suggests the imagery that God's temple is made up of living stones from every people—Jews and gentile nations alike (see 2 Corinthians 6:16; Ephesians 2:11–22; 1 Peter 2:5). Since many believers today patronizingly insist that it is not the time for God to finish building this temple made without hands, and since many believers are sequestering most of God's blessings to pad their own nests, try to read Haggai's message without flinching:

> "Thus says the Lord of hosts,
> 'This people says, "The time has not come, even the time for the house of the Lord to be rebuilt." ' "

Then the word of the Lord came by Haggai the prophet saying,
"Is it time for you yourselves to dwell in your paneled houses while
this house lies desolate?"
Now therefore, thus says the Lord of hosts,
"Consider your ways!
You have sown much, but harvest little;
You eat, but there is not enough to be satisfied;
You drink, but there is not enough to become drunk;
You put on clothing, but no one is warm enough;
And he who earns, earns wages to put into a purse with holes. . . .
You look for much, but behold, it comes to little;
When you bring it home, I blow it away.
Why? . . . Because of My house which lies desolate,
While each of you runs to his own house." (Haggai 1:2–9)

Happily, God's people "obeyed the voice of the Lord their God . . ." and "showed reverence for the Lord." God reminded them, "I am with you," and "stirred up . . . the spirit of all the remnant of the people; and they came and worked on the house of the Lord of hosts, their God" (Haggai 1:12–14). And as they worked to finally finish the temple four years later, they doubtless remembered God's promise: "Surely there is a future, and your hope will not be cut off" (Proverbs 23:18). Their repentance didn't simply include a renouncing of sins; it also incorporated a return to God's clear purpose to finish building His temple.

If God's people repent merely to receive more of God's blessing for themselves, nothing happens. The land isn't healed. If God's people repent to receive more of God's "top-line" blessing in order to pass on "bottom-line" blessings to every people, God's response is immediate: "Take courage . . . and work, for I am with you. . . . My Spirit is abiding in your midst; do not fear!" (Haggai 2:4, 5).

Devout Men From Every Nation

Later, God orchestrated events in the lives of Ezra and Nehemiah to go back and rebuild the walls of Jerusalem. Why? God predicted through Jeremiah: "Behold, I will bring to [Jerusalem] health and healing, and I will heal them; and I will reveal to them an abundance of peace and truth." And why would God again bless His people in the rebuilt Jerusalem? "And it shall be to Me a name of joy, praise, and glory before all the nations of the earth, which shall hear of all the good that I do for them" (Jeremiah 33:6, 9).

God accomplishes His purpose and, whether His people are willing to align themselves with that purpose or not, "He does according to His will in the host of heaven"—as He retakes Satan's counter-kingdom in the spiritual realm—"and among the inhabitants of earth" as He brings men to himself through salvation (Daniel 4:35).

Even among those of God's people who stayed in Babylon rather than return to Jerusalem, God pushed His agenda during the dispersion. The sweeping-saga scenes of the book of Esther have but one point: God broadcasts His powerful, redeeming character through the "satraps, the governors, and the princes of the provinces which extended from India [which some scholars say referred to everything east of Babylon!] to Ethiopia [which probably meant a good portion of the continent of Africa], 127 provinces, to every province according to its script, and to every people according to their language" (Esther 8:9).

God made sure that even these Jewish exiles clearly proclaimed "words of peace and truth" (Esther 9:30)—topics of God's blessing and character—so that all peoples could respond: "In each and every province, and in each and every city . . . many among the peoples of the land became Jews" and "allied themselves with them" (Esther 8:17; 9:27).

In the ensuing 400 years until the birth of the Light, "Thy salvation, [God] prepared in the presence of all peoples" (Luke 2:30–32), the number of God's people grew among the nations. Jewish missions to win proselytes (converts from other peoples who completely followed all Jewish rites) and "God-fearers" (converts who believed but were not circumcised) prospered until there were at the time of the early apostles "devout men, from every nation under heaven" (Acts 2:5)!

God propels His purpose to offer salvation to every people, tribe, tongue and nation—whether His people want to be blessed in the process or not!

To Whom Much Is Given

God has overwhelmingly blessed His people worldwide. In 1990, it was reported that:

- Globally there are 1.2 billion people who call themselves Christians and who share their faith.

- There are 500 million Christians committed to acting on the mandate to "bless all the peoples"—sometimes called "Great Commission Christians." This number grows at an average rate of 6.9% per year, which is faster than the global population rate. For example, while world population has doubled since 1950, the number of Great Commission Christians has grown more than six times in the same period.
- About 100 million evangelical believers worldwide are young people. Just one-tenth of 1% of these would field a force of 100,000 new missionaries—the mission force needed to send church-planting teams to each of the remaining unreached people groups.
- Worldwide, Great Commission Christians earn $2.5 trillion in disposable income. We give about $8 billion annually to missions—about one-third of 1% of our disposable income. To send a mission force of an additional 100,000 to the unreached peoples of the world would require about $1.25 billion more—about one-twentieth of one percent.
- There are 7 million Great Commission churches in 23,500 denominations in the world. This means there are about 583 congregations that could adopt each remaining unreached people group for prayer, giving and sending missionaries.
- The world is home to about 170 million believers who daily pray for salvation to come to all people groups. For example, the city of Boroko, Papua New Guinea, is home base for the Global Prayer Warriors organization directed by Walo Ani.
- Twenty million believers are engaged in full-time prayer ministries.
- There are at least 3 million full-time Great Commission workers.
- Thirty thousand Christians work full-time in broadcasting the Gospel in cross-cultural mission efforts. About 4.6 billion of the world's population receive Gospel radio broadcasts in their own mother tongue.
- Twenty-five thousand are involved in leadership positions in Great Commission efforts to bless every nation with the Gospel.
- Christians own more than 60 million computers—many of which are linked in 4,000 global computer networks, 36 worldwide intercessory networks, 56 global networks, 9 global mega-networks

and one immense Great Commission giga-network tying together all the information Christians can gather about each of the remaining unreached people groups.

- There are at this time 3,970 mission agencies, 285,250 career missionaries, 180,000 short-term missionaries and 400 Great Commission research centers worldwide. One thousand of the mission agencies are new Third World organizations.
- There are more than 2,000 global plans to evangelize the world in operation as of 1990. All of these current plans have embarked in some sense on a countdown process involving the years 1990–2000. As of year-end 1990, two-thirds of these plans were making active progress.
- Annually 2,500 mass evangelism campaigns broadcast the Gospel.
- More than 11,000 evangelistic items are produced each year; about 23,800 Christian periodicals proclaim the Good News; over 51 million Bibles are distributed yearly.[2]

What do you think? Has God given His people the blessings and the resources to actively be a blessing to all the remaining unreached people groups of the earth?

Other blessings aren't quite so obvious since they're not necessarily quantified statistics. For example, the fact that we can travel to any point in the world within 24 hours is a phenomenon allowed mankind in just the past couple of decades.

Much of the Western world has been blessed with old age. The "graying of America," for example, is a tremendous resource for implementing God's plan to bless every people with the offer of salvation. As rest homes and nursing facilities expand with record numbers of the elderly, some see longer lifespans as a curse of boredom and uselessness. But a worldview that focuses on God's unchangeable purpose sees the growing population of elderly believers as a significant resource expressly allowed by God for such a time as this.

The elderly can still work at reaching the world. At the time of Christ, the average lifespan was 28 years—which was not much time to grow up, get educated, have a family and figure out how to practically

---

[2]Statistics from Lausanne Statistics Task Force as published in David Barrett and Todd Johnson's *Our Globe and How to Reach It*, New Hope Publishers, Birmingham, Alabama, 1990, and the 1990 *Unreached Peoples Poster*, the U.S. Center for World Mission, Pasadena, California.

focus on God's plan for the nations. Today's lifespan in the West is nearly three times that figure. Today's believer has three times the number of years of growth and maturity to fight the good fight in the process of proclaiming the excellencies of His name.

The elderly can wage spiritual warfare as they pray around the world. Since the remaining unreached peoples are still held captive under the strongholds of Satan, prayer power is critical to finishing the task. Even culturally sensitive proclamations of the Gospel are unheard in an unreached people because the "god of this world" and his minions are hard at work solidifying their positions of rulership by "blinding minds" (2 Corinthians 4:4). No other population segment of Christians has more discretionary time for serious, global prayer than the experienced, mature elderly!

God has blessed His people.

What are we doing with His resources? Running to panel our own houses while God builds His temple of living stones the "hard way?"

In the U.S., the picture is pretty bleak. According to the *Bibles for All World Prayer Map*, American Christians spend 95% of offerings on home-based ministry, 4.5% on cross-cultural efforts in already reached people groups, and 0.5% to reach the unreached.

Selah. (That's an Old Testament term meaning "Pause and meditate.")

*H*ours later as the sun sets over the distant coast of Tanzania, you restlessly fall asleep with a couple of lines from an old song running through your mind: "God bless America, land that I love. . . ."

For Further Thought

1. Write out in your own words David's song from 1 Chronicles 16:18, 23, 24, 28, 29, 31.
2. Reread Haggai 1. Review the lists of blessings God has bestowed on His people and on America as a culture. Then, as long as your knees can stand it, pray for God's people to recognize the purpose of God's blessings.
3. As long as their knees allow, your friends need to be challenged to pray in a new way for America. Suggest that they not pray that God would heal our land so that we can have a nicer, safer life. If your prayer group has a vision for what God can do for America, that's

wonderful; but America is only 6% of God's heart! Our prayers that God would heal our land should be to the end that we use the incredible resources He has poured out on us for His purpose—to bless *every* people.

CHAPTER 8

A Messiah for All Peoples: A Race Through the New Testament

*B*ritisher Clarence Duncan met you at the harbor patrol customs office and has bounced you over miles of dusty grassland driving east from the coast in Tanzania. The top of the LandRover is open, and fine silt puffs each time you shift in your seat. It's a bright, hot day, and the breeze is so welcome you close your eyes and rest your head back as Clarence fights the wheel and the Rover bounces comfortably over the dirt road.

This is an unusual man. God has put him in an unusual place: in the middle of a solidly Islamic country in the middle of a solidly Islamic people group—the Yao. The Yao live in Tanzania, Mozambique, Malawi and a few other southeastern African countries. Clarence has told you how he arrived in a village when he first came in 1985.

He had called a meeting with the village chief and elders, sat before them and gone through the customary pleasantries. Then the chief asked, "What is your name?" We've learned the importance of names in the non-Western cultures of the world, right?

Clarence had simply answered, "Mr. Clarence."

The council looked at each other. The chief asked, "Why are you here?"

Again very simply, Clarence had answered, "I want to tell your people about *Isa Al Mahsi.*" And permission was immediately granted.

Now Clarence is explaining over the roar of the Rover: "Then a couple months later when the chief had realized he could trust me, he said, 'Do you know why we allowed you to stay?' And I said, 'Never thought about it.' He said, 'Twenty-one years ago a very old Yao man came to our village and called for a meeting as you did. When we asked

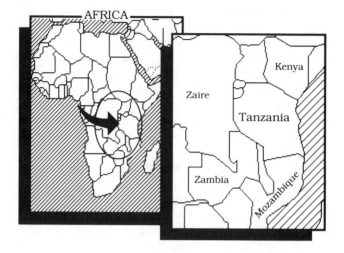

him his name, this Yao man said, "Mr. Clarence"—which isn't an African name at all! When we asked him why he came, he said, "I want to tell your people about *Isa Al Mahsi*." These were your very words. Twenty-one years ago Mr. Clarence led four of our villagers to follow Jesus. So we ran them out of the village. And we killed Mr. Clarence. The reason we allowed you to stay was we were afraid.' "

Then Clarence's British lilt rolls right into another story that took place just two years ago. Yao were coming to Christ, and a church had been planted. The Islamic authorities in the region tried to deport him and his family, but God intervened. Then he hits you with another one of those goose-bump revelations of the way God is orchestrating events all over the globe to bless every people group with redemption in Christ.

Clarence says:

> One January morning, I think it was the fourteenth, about ten in the morning, up our driveway comes a whole retinue of 24 Muslim leaders from around the country. The whole country! Behind them many of the people from our village followed to watch what was obviously going to be some sort of public spectacle. I didn't want that, so I asked the Muslim leaders to send the people away and I would do so with the Christians. After some discussion they agreed.
>
> After the greetings and our meal together, we all sat down in a

large rectangular room adjacent to our house. I was against one wall, 23 of the Muslim leaders along the other walls. The head of the leaders sat in the middle of the room opposite me.

He said they had come to ask me a few questions about the Christian faith.

"That's fine," I said, "but so that you will know the answers to your questions are not things I invent, I will read the answers from the Bible." I gave them each a Bible in the trade language and told them where they could read along with me before I read a passage.

The head sheik sitting opposite me began the questioning. The others sat silently observing.

The first question was "Why do you Christians say that there are three gods?" The answer was a simple one. I told them the page number for Deuteronomy 6:4: "Hear, O Israel! The LORD is our God, the Lord is one! And you shall love the Lord your God with all your heart, and with all your soul and with all your might." And I mentioned to them that these are the words *Isa* (Jesus) quoted when He spoke to the scribes in Mark 12:29, regarding the "greatest commandment." Jesus himself told us there is one God.

The barrage of questions went on until about lunchtime when the meeting was suddenly adjourned. They went outside for their Friday noon prayers and then came back in for more questions.

As the afternoon wore on, the leader kept asking more questions. There was one question about the Trinity that was hard for me to answer using Scripture alone. I wanted to explain it in a graphic, visual way. But in order to do that I had to stand up, walk around and gesture.

About five o'clock in the afternoon, they abruptly decided the meeting was over and left.

The one who had asked all the questions, Sheik Abu Bakr, hung back until we were alone in the room. He said quietly, "Would you come see me next week?" I nodded, and he left.

When I saw him the next week he looked at me carefully and asked, "Do you know why we came to visit you last week?"

A bit puzzled by the question, I answered, "Certainly. You came to ask me questions about the Christian faith."

"No," Abu said, "we came to kill you."

In the African culture, you never tell someone you intend to hurt him, to say nothing of having intentions to kill him!

Abu continued, "Do you remember when a group tried to throw

you out of the country—and it didn't work? The Christian church here grew so much we Muslim leaders knew we had to get you out one way or another. We decided that the only way was to kill you.

"We spent three days consulting our witchcraft as to how we would do this before we came to see you. Finally we decided on our plan: We would each sit in a specific place in the room, with our medicine in our pocket. We had even invited the people of the village to watch what would happen. When we asked you questions our magic would be so powerful you would be struck dumb and would not be able to answer the questions. Then you would be laughed at and humiliated. And after a while, you would fall to the ground paralyzed, and then die.

"But when we asked you the first question, you kept talking and talking and talking! We thought, 'Our medicine isn't working.' When we went out in the middle of the day, we consulted our magic again and came in and sat in different places to improve the power. But still it would not work.

"Do you remember when you explained to us the Trinity? You got up and walked around, waving your arms, and talking and talking! After that we decided you had a more powerful Spirit who was protecting you. So we decided there was no use trying to kill you and gave up and left."

Needless to say I was quite surprised to hear this story.

Abu broke into my thoughts, "I want to become a Christian."

Well, that shocked me more than anything! I said, "Why?" And the sheik told me this story.

"When I was a teenager, in our village we were not Muslim people and we were not Christian. We were Achewa people with our own religion. Behind our village was a hill where I would often go to pray.

"One day I was on that hill praying. Suddenly all around me was a blinding light. Out of this light I saw a big hand coming toward me holding an open book. I looked at the book and saw writing on the page. A Voice told me to read. I protested that I could not read, never having been to school. The Voice again told me to read. So I did. And suddenly the book and the hand disappeared.

"I ran back to my village and all the people were looking for me, thinking I had died on that hill! They asked about a fire they had seen up there. When I told them the story they laughed at me saying, 'You can't read!'

"Someone got a book and I began to read! Then people came from all around to find out more about what happened and ask questions. The Muslim authorities found out about me and I was trained in the ways of Islam. Soon all of our village became Muslim. For 15 years I was the greatest debater against the Christians."

He paused and I asked him, "Why are you telling me all of this?"

He said, "You remember when I asked you the first question about why Christians believe in three gods? Your answer was Deuteronomy chapter six, verse four."

"That's right," I said.

Sheik Abu Bakr looked me straight in the eye and said, "That was the same passage that this Voice on the mountain showed me. At that moment I knew that the God you were talking about was the True God!"

Talk about a shock! I asked, "Then why did you keep asking me all those questions the whole day?"

"Because," he smiled, "I wanted all these Muslim leaders to know what the Christians believe and I wanted them to hear it from you. The whole day I pretended unbelief so that I could ask more questions. Now I want to become a Christian."

You're not even near the Duncan's village yet; but you've been blessed by what God is doing among the Yao. And you're also jealous: Wouldn't it be wonderful to be used by God so specifically in His great plan to bless a people group! Then you realize you're getting the idea. God's historic Great Commission given to Abraham 4,000 years ago does include you, your life, your place in history. God can use every believer just as wonderfully as He has the Duncans! But how?

The apostle Paul says that "to each one of us grace ["giftedness" is an accurate synonym] was given according to the measure of Christ's gift. And He gave some as apostles, and some as prophets, and some as evangelists, and some as pastors and teachers, for the equipping of the saints for the work of service—" For what purpose? "to the building up of the Body of Christ" (Ephesians 4:7, 11, 12).

We each have a function, a place (see Romans 12:3-8; 1 Corinthians 12). Paul writes, "All are not apostles, are they?" (1 Corinthians 12:29). Apostle means "sent one"; and you simply weren't sent to the Yao. At least not at this point. Your mandate is to fulfill your role in the Body now so it can function, "being fitted and held together . . . according to the proper working of each individual part" (Ephesians 4:16).

And what is the Body of Christ doing? It's going about the Father's business! It is building itself up as a temple of living stones. It's being blessed to be a blessing to every people on the earth. At least, you're thinking, most of the Body seems to be moving in the direction of God's unchangeable purpose. And you wonder uneasily why the Body is moving so miraculously and growing in every part of the world except in Western Europe and North America!

Perhaps some of the reason is that we, like Israel, read even our New Testaments with an eye only for God's top-line blessing on ourselves. What does the New Testament say about this ongoing Story of the Bible? Is Jesus the Messiah for all peoples?

Our meager glimpse at the Old Testament's solid predictions of Christ as the Servant who "will sprinkle many nations" (Isaiah 52:15) has at least prepared us to take a fresh glance at the familiarity of the New Testament. Is God's unchangeable purpose an obvious theme running through the next 26 sections of the Story of the Bible? Let's race through the New Testament.

The Gospels

Jesus was born as a light to the gentiles.

- John the Baptist was celebrated at birth as the forerunner of the Christ who was coming to "shine upon those who sit in darkness and the shadow of death" (Luke 1:79). Anyone listening to this song of Zacharias's knew the passage in Isaiah referred to God making Galilee of the gentiles glorious by the coming of the Messiah (see Isaiah 9). Remember the term "gentile" means every people group other than Jews.
- Likewise, Simeon's announcement of Jesus' birth clearly confirmed the all-nations scope of the Messiah: "For my eyes have seen Thy salvation, which Thou hast prepared in the presence of all peoples, a light of revelation to the gentiles, and the glory of Thy people Israel" (Luke 2:30–32). Simeon also quoted from Isaiah: "I will also make You a light of the nations so that My salvation may reach to the end of the earth" (Isaiah 49:6).
- This same passage is repeated later as Paul and Barnabus arrived in the town of Pisidian Antioch to spread the blessing (Acts 13:13–52).

After the reading of the Law and the Prophets in the synagogue, Paul proclaimed the all-nations message of God to the "sons of Abraham's family and those among them who fear God." Paul presented the fact that the Christ had died and rose again to provide salvation for "everyone who believes"—not just the Jews. He warned his Jewish listeners not to scoff at the blessing being offered to everyone; then he quoted Habakkuk 1:5, "Look among the nations! Observe! Be astonished! Wonder! Because *I* am doing something in your days—You would not believe if you were told."

When the following Sabbath brought retaliation from jealous Jews, Paul and Barnabus replied they were following God's explicit command. They simply quoted the verse Simeon shouted at Jesus' birth: "I have placed You as a light for the Gentiles that You should bring salvation to the end of the earth" (Acts 13:47; Isaiah 49:6). The result? The word of the Lord was being spread throughout the whole region!

Jesus' early ministry was to the Jew first but also to all peoples.

Jesus could have made His headquarters the center of Judaism in Jerusalem. Instead, He initially based His ministry in Galilee of the gentiles. His first miracle was in Cana. In His first sermon in Nazareth (Luke 4:24–30), He reminded His Jewish and gentile audience that the great faith He called men to was best exemplified in those from other people groups:

Elijah was sent to a widow woman of the Sidon people (1 Kings 17).

Naaman, a Syrian military officer whose people were mercilessly destroying Israel at that very time, was healed of leprosy because of the intercession of a little Israeli servant-girl (2 Kings 5:1–14).

- In His hometown area of "Galilee of the gentiles," Jesus "seeing the multitudes . . . felt compassion for them. . . . Then He said to His disciples, 'The harvest is plentiful, but the workers are few. Therefore beseech the Lord of the harvest to send out workers into His harvest" (Matthew 9:36–38; see the parallel passage in Luke 10:2.) His heart not only yearns for His people; God feels compassion for the multitudes of every people group on earth.

  An incisive translation of the phrase "send out" is "thrust out" or even "cast out!" It is the same verb used when Jesus drove out the temple moneychangers and cast out demons. Sometimes God's action in getting laborers active in His harvest will be a bit disconcerting—even painful—to the "thrust-out" workers!

As Jack McAlister of the World Prayer 2000 ministry says, Jesus promised two problems in the worldwide harvest: The harvest will be vast and the workers will be few. His answer? Pray!

- When Jesus sent out the twelve, He strategically commanded them to go to the "lost sheep of Israel" (see Matthew 10). Warning the nation of impending judgment, the disciples were not to spend time in what they later would do—preaching to other peoples. Even in that context of Israel's doom, however, the disciples were to be aware that every other people would be watching how God handled His reputation among His people: "You shall even be brought before governors and kings for My sake, as a testimony to them and to the gentiles" (Matthew 10:18).

Later, Jesus sent out the seventy disciples (Luke 10:1–20) to every city He would visit—whether Jewish or not. First, twelve, possibly representing the twelve tribes of Israel, were sent exclusively to the Jews to warn that nation of judgment. Then 70, possibly representing the 70 nations formed at the Tower of Babel, were sent out to call all people groups to repentance.

Jesus' later ministry included all peoples.

Jesus later spent His time in Jewish areas. So it is noteworthy that so many of His contacts were with individuals of other peoples:

- He healed the Gadarene demoniac (Matthew 8:28–34).
- He noted that a Samaritan was the only one of ten lepers who returned to thank Him for healing them (Luke 17:12–19).
- He explained to a Samaritan woman that God was to be worshiped in spirit and in truth (John 4:5–42).
- A Canaanite woman's daughter was released from demon-possession because of the mother's great faith (Matthew 15:22–28). Reading this remarkable passage carefully, we see that Jesus' initial silence and statement of exclusivity ("I was sent only to . . . Israel") was totally out of character for the One born the Light of the gentiles. We can almost sense His, and the woman's, facetiousness as Jesus taught His prejudiced disciples (see verse

23) a critical lesson: God is interested in freeing all peoples from the powers of Satan's counter-kingdom.

- The Roman centurion's servant was healed as Jesus marveled at his faith (Matthew 8:5–13). Jesus reminded His audience that "many shall come from east and west, and recline at the table with Abraham, and Isaac, and Jacob, in the kingdom of heaven."
- A group of Greek God-fearers pleaded with Philip, "Sir, we wish to see Jesus." And it was to this group Jesus first announced clearly His coming death: "And I, if I be lifted up from the earth, will draw all men to Myself" (John 12:21, 32). All men.

In the final events of His life on earth, Jesus acted on behalf of every people.

Events from the last week before Jesus' crucifixion to His ascension teem with references to the all-nations theme of the Story of the Bible:

- Christ entered Jerusalem "humble, and mounted on a donkey," fulfilling the prophecy that there would come a king who would "speak peace to the nations; and His dominion will be from sea to sea . . . to the ends of the earth" (Zechariah 9:9, 10).
- Jesus cleansed the temple's court of the gentiles, throwing out the hawkers and moneychangers, and saying, "Is it not written, 'My house shall be called a house of prayer for all the nations'?" (Mark 11:17).
- The final week before the cross is when He answered clearly the question, "What will be the sign of Your coming, and of the end of the age?" His answer? Jesus tells of several "birth pangs," and then says, "This gospel of the kingdom shall be preached in the whole world for a witness to all the nations, and then the end shall come" (Matthew 24:3–14).
- As Mary anointed Jesus at the house in Bethany, Jesus promised that every people would hear of her devotion "wherever this gospel is preached in the whole world" (Matthew 26:13).
- Let us never forget the global significance of Jesus' death for the sins of the whole world (1 John 2:2). "For God so loved the world, that He gave His only begotten Son, that whoever believes in Him should not perish, but have eternal life" (John 3:16).
- After His resurrection, Jesus patiently explained the whole of Scripture to the two disciples on the road to Emmaus and later to

all the disciples (Luke 24:13–49). His nutshell commentary included all nations:

He opened their minds to understand the Scriptures and He said to them,

> Thus it is written, that the Christ should suffer and rise again from the dead the third day; and that repentance for forgiveness of sins should be proclaimed in His name to all the nations beginning from Jerusalem." (Luke 24:46, 47)

How clear can the Story of the Bible be? Forgiveness of sins should be proclaimed in His name to all the nations!

* As Jesus met for the final time with His disciples in Galilee of the gentiles, He gave what we have called the Great Commission. By now we know that this command was nothing new. It was not simply an afterthought of what the disciples could do with their spare time until He returned. This command was a clear, forceful repetition of the message God had been giving since His imperative 2,000 years before when He had told Abraham, "And so you shall be a blessing. . . . And in you all the families of the earth shall be blessed" (Genesis 12:2, 3).

Acknowledging this familiar passage as the Great Re-Commission, let's think carefully through what Jesus actually said:

"All authority has been given to Me in heaven and on earth" (Matthew 28:18). Jesus has disarmed all rulers and authorities in the heavenly realm of Satan's battling counter-kingdom (Colossians 2:15, and Hebrews 2:14–15). The peoples of the earth no longer have to be prisoners of Satan's darkness. They remain enslaved only because of ignorance of Christ's freedom, or because of obstinance in deference to Satan.

Because of the "therefore" (Matthew 28:19), we are commanded to make disciples. The "go" in this passage is not actually an imperative in the Greek text; it is more accurately an assumption: "As you are going. . . ." The force of the entire text is the command "make disciples"—followers, learners.

What is the object of the command? "Every *ethne*"—all the peoples/nations/gentiles/families of the earth. The 1611 King James Version of the Bible, the solid version used for centuries in the English-speaking world, translated this phrase "teach all nations." What complicated the King James Version of the Great Re-Commission, of course, was its parallel passage in Mark 16:15: "Go ye into all the world and preach the Gospel to every creature." No wonder many Western Christians think Christ's command is only idealism; telling the Gospel to *every individual* on earth is a hopeless task!

But the original texts are clear: Jesus reminded us of the mandate given Abraham centuries before: reach every people group. Then, equip those who respond by baptizing them into the name of the Father, Son and Holy Spirit, and teaching them to observe all that Christ commanded—including this command!

Then, just as God reminded Jacob (Genesis 28:15—with the exact wording in the Greek Septuagint version of the Old Testament), the God-Man said, "Lo, I am with you."

The Acts of the Apostles

As usual, the disciples were stuck on top-line blessing as they asked the ascending Christ, "Lord, is it at this time You are restoring the kingdom to Israel?" (Acts 1:6). In other words, "Are we now going to get the whole bundle of blessings promised us as God's chosen people?"

Jesus, of course, replies with a clear-cut statement that balances top-line blessing: "It is not for you to know times or epochs which the Father has fixed by His own authority; but you shall receive power when the Holy Spirit has come upon you—" and bottom-line responsibility: "and you shall be My witnesses both in Jerusalem, and in all Judea and Samaria, and even to the remotest part of the earth" (Acts 1:6–8).

The remainder of the Acts of the Apostles can be seen in light of this: God's blessing on His people to bless all peoples.

The Day of Pentecost modeled the plan.

You're in Jerusalem. You're one of the God-fearers who by faith is trusting in the God of the Jews. You're fresh off the ship from Cnidus in Phrygia—in what would later become western Turkey.

Seasickness was nothing compared to the disorientation you feel amid the rush of dusty travelers and locals weaving in and out among each other in the crowd-packed walkways of the market. Children shriek in a language foreign to you, some bright-robed market hawkers shout, "Melons! Fresh melons!" in Greek, the language you've learned to worship in back home at the synagogue.

But the conversations, the remarks and shouts all around you as you wade through the striped-robed crowd are in languages you've never heard before. You constantly remind yourself that no matter how foreign you feel in this place, they're not really all talking about you.

Suddenly a wild windstorm blows in off the desert, but protected here in the market alleyways, you don't even feel a puff of wind.

Then you hear it wafting above the tumult: Up at the next corner a man is standing on the back of a cart speaking in pure, unaccented Phrygian.

You rush forward, to get a closer look. Could it be that other God-fearers from your homeland are here too? Now you see that most of the marketplace crowd is surging toward the same corner, everyone speaking in a different language. It is an effort to see above the milling turbans of dozens of men. Women are also gathering around, and finally you are close enough to notice the swarthy features of the man—he is a Jew! He's explaining that the promise of God's long-awaited blessing has now come to you!

"Repent and let each of you be baptized in the name of Jesus Christ for the forgiveness of your sins; and you shall receive the gift of the Holy Spirit. For the promise is for you and your children, and for all who are far off . . ." (Acts 2:38, 39).

You know that you are one whom the Scriptures refer to as "far off." The promise of the Abrahamic blessing has come to you!

Then the bottom-line hits you. If you and any other Phrygians here today are the first to hear of this fulfillment, who is responsible for carrying the news of this blessing back home?

So Pentecost demonstrated God's blessing on His people, the disciples on whom the power of the promised Spirit fell, and on every nation. The Day of Pentecost proclaimed the fact that God's blessing was to drench "devout men from every nation under heaven"—and apparently all the nations were represented in the one city of Jerusalem at that incredible point in history (Acts 2:5). God showed that the New Testament plan was the same as the Old: God blesses His people to be a blessing to every people.

The early sermons hinged on God's outpouring of blessing on the Jew first, and also on all peoples.

- In the days following Pentecost, the headstrong fisherman Simon Peter eloquently articulated the order of God's blessing in a sermon to the Jewish crowd gathered at the portico of Solomon, a porch along the temple's Court of the Gentiles:

"All the prophets . . . announced these days, 'It is you who are the sons of the prophets, and of the covenant which God made with your fathers, saying to Abraham, "And in your seed all the families of the earth shall be blessed." For you first, God raised up His Servant and sent Him to bless you by turning every one of you from your wicked ways' " (Acts 3:24–26). God's people were blessed to be a blessing.

- The apostle Paul, speaking years later in a synagogue in Phrygia, confirms this order: "It was necessary that the Word of God would be spoken to you first; since . . . 'I have placed you as a light for the gentiles' " (Acts 13:46, 47).

As usual, God's people—even the venerated early disciples—hesitated to bless the nations.

- Jerusalem was the most strategic, central place to reach the people group called the Jews. So, although it was not home to most of the early disciples, that is where they focused their early ministry of passing on the blessing.

    Christ orders us to expend the power of the Spirit by being witnesses in strategic places within our own people group. Be careful if someone's interpretation of Jesus' command to "be witnesses" suggests that no shift, no movement, no change of lifestyle is necessary to become an obedient disciple. Jesus always prods us out of the status quo.

    Also, Jesus had told the disciples to be witnesses to Him "both" in Jerusalem and beyond—not first in Jerusalem, and then when they had things well under control there, to the ends of the earth.

- But, as Jonah of old, the disciples would not budge. And God initiated His age-old motivation system to bless all nations whether His people cooperated voluntarily or not. "A great persecution arose against the church in Jerusalem." And the predictable result? "They were all scattered throughout the regions of Judea and Samaria." The Lord sent them exactly where He said He would—"into all Judea and Samaria." Why? To accomplish His unchangeable purpose: "Therefore those who had been scattered went about preaching the word" (Acts 8:1, 4).

The infamous Cultural Revolution in the People's Republic of China in the 1960's and 1970's parallels this persecution account in the book of Acts. Beginning in the 1960's, the Chinese Communist Party "purged" their culture of millions of intellectuals and Western-influenced citizens. Tens of thousands of these persecuted people were Christians, and as they were forcibly relocated or as they fled from China's cities to remote, rural areas, they carried the Gospel with them.

Before the time of the Cultural Revolution, it was estimated that there were about 2,000 unreached people groups within the political borders of China. But after 1976 when China opened somewhat to the West, researchers were astounded to find that possibly 1,000 of these unreached people groups had been reached with the Gospel during these terrible years of persecution. God had spread His Word from people group to people group through persecution.

- Notice that Philip was one of those scattered. He's probably the classic example of God drafting someone into His great Cause. Especially if you're a deacon in a local church, watch and tremble at Philip's progress in aligning with God's purpose to bless the nations:

  Philip is chosen to be a local church deacon (Acts 6:5).

  Philip is pushed into being a cross-cultural evangelist (Acts 8:5). Samaritans were considered to be half-Jewish and half-Assyrian, so Philip's preaching had to cross some cultural barriers of custom and acceptance. But as he preached in his own language to this culturally near people, his ministry would be considered at this point to be evangelism—sharing the Gospel within your own or a culturally similar people group.

  Philip is thrust out into the Gaza desert to proclaim Christ as the suffering Servant of Isaiah to the Ethiopian eunuch (Acts 8:26–39). And as he explained the Word beginning at Isaiah 53, he undoubtedly kept on reading and explaining until the Nubian was spellbound to hear:

  Let not the foreigner who has joined himself to the Lord say, "The Lord will surely separate me from His people." Neither let the eunuch say, "Behold, I am a dry tree." For thus says the Lord, "To the eunuchs who keep my sabbaths, and choose what pleases Me . . . to them I will

give in My house and within My walls a memorial, and a
name better than that of sons and daughters; I will give
them an everlasting name which will not be cut off. . . .
Their burnt offerings and their sacrifices will be acceptable
on My altar; for My house will be called a house of prayer
for all the peoples." (Isaiah 56:3–7)

Would it be any wonder if the eunuch suddenly whistled his
chariot to a stop and exclaimed, "Why didn't they tell me this
back at the synagogue? I thought God loved the Jews more than
any other people! I thought I had to renounce my whole cultural
heritage to become acceptable to the God of Abraham, Isaac and
Jacob!" Actually, he said, "Look! Water! What prevents me from
being baptized?" (Acts 8:36).

And so Philip was drawn by God through the training of serving as a deacon and an evangelist to eventually bless another
people. As he reached across distinct cultural barriers to the Nubian, Philip fulfilled a mission. He was a missionary to another
people group. And the Good News spread into Africa.

- After the whole theme of Old Testament Scripture, after Jesus'
ministry and final words to keep passing on the blessing, the
Apostles were still reluctant to believe God was longing to bless
the gentiles as well as the Jews.

Even after Peter's all-nations sermon just after Pentecost, he
needed a distinct vision from God to offer the Good News to the
gentile family of Cornelius (Acts 10). Three times God reminded
Peter in the vision that His unchangeable plan was to bless His
people in order to bless every nation. As if thumped over the head
with the message of the vision, Peter says, "I most certainly
understand now that God is not one to show partiality but in every
ethne the man who fears Him and does what is right, is welcome
to Him" (Acts 10:34, 35).

The other disciples' response to the Caesarean non-Jews' salvation in Christ? Rejoicing? Excitement that God's obvious plan
since Genesis 12:3 was unfolding before their very eyes? No, they
"took issue" with Peter. Peter shrugged, "Who was I that I could
stand in God's way?" Then the noble, respected-throughout-his-
tory early disciples "when they heard this, they quieted down and
glorified God, saying, 'Well then, God has granted to the Gentiles
also the repentance that leads to life' " (Acts 11:18). But they

didn't give up their top-line grasp easily.

- A whole council had to be called to iron out more of this unnerving business of God having His way in blessing other people groups! At the Council of Jerusalem years after Pentecost (Acts 15), the Jewish-based church was still mostly concerned about itself.

    Peter tried another run at convincing the Jerusalem leadership that God had indeed intended that the Great Commission be taken literally, that "He made no distinction between us and them" (Acts 15:9). James had to appeal to Scripture to break through: "God first concerned Himself about taking from among the Gentiles a people for His name and with this the words of the prophets agree . . . 'I will rebuild the tabernacle of David . . . in order that the rest of mankind may seek the Lord, and all the Gentiles who are called by My name' " (Acts 15:14–17).

    Under James, the physical brother of Jesus, the early church leadership finally grasped the idea that God would accomplish His will to bless every people on earth. And who were they, that they could stand in God's way?

The Epistles

The Epistles of the New Testament are familiar to most believers as rich ground for understanding doctrine and growing in Christ.

Christian growth has a distinct earthly purpose.

Within the light of the theme of the Story of the Bible, we have to ask ourselves, "Why work at understanding doctrine and growing in Christ?"

Maybe we would automatically answer, "So our lives will be better" or "To become more like Christ." Both of these answers are true. Partially.

But if God simply wanted us to know doctrine "even as we are known," to no longer "see through a glass darkly," to be "holy and blameless before Him," wouldn't it make sense to swoop us away from the sludge of sin and the irritations of life in a fallen, Satan-plagued earth?

Or does God have a very distinct purpose for leaving us on earth? A custom-designed niche for us to fill in His unchangeable purpose?

And doesn't it make sense that, since God uses humans in His plan,

He wants us clean and equipped and obedient?

God admonishes us to be students of the Word, to rightly divide the Word of truth, not so that we'll be able to speak it out from memory, but so that we will be transformed by it and use it to transform others! God orders husbands and wives to learn to live with each other according to knowledge and to love each other not so they'll have rosy, glorious lives on beds of ease and prosperity; strong marriages are essential for a Christian couple to tackle the strongholds of Satan in order to work toward God's unchangeable purposes. God asks us to bear one another's burdens so we can get on with the task at hand. God instructs us to conduct ourselves with holiness and propriety not so we'll feel superior or lead charmed lives, but so that His name will be exalted among the world's *ethne*.

God wants us to know why He is gracious to us, why He blesses us and causes His face to shine upon us: so that His way may be known on the earth, His salvation among all peoples (Psalm 67:1, 2).

The meat of the epistles is not intended for our blessing alone. The primary reason for Paul's deep doctrinal and practical teaching is what sets apart his epistle to the Romans.

At the beginning of the book he writes, "Paul, a bond-servant of Christ Jesus . . . through whom we have received grace and apostleship to bring about the obedience of faith among all the Gentiles, for His name's sake . . . to all who are beloved of God in Rome" (Romans 1:1, 5, 7).

Near the end of his letter, Paul shares the vision of his life: "Thus I aspired to preach the gospel, not where Christ was already named . . . but as it is written, 'They who had no news of Him shall see, and they who have not heard shall understand' " (Romans 15:20, 21).

And at the very end, Paul reemphasizes the reason why the teaching is critical. The Spirit wanted the Roman believers to be established firmly in the (1) "gospel and the preaching of Jesus Christ," and (2) "the revelation of the mystery which has been kept secret . . . but now is manifested, and by the Scriptures of the prophets" which had "been made known to all the nations leading to obedience of faith" (Romans 16:25, 26).

The epistles are written to bless us with wisdom and strength because God has a distinct job for each of us. And in some indirect or direct way, it has to do with the people groups of our era who have not been blessed with the offer of salvation in Jesus Christ.

Christian growth prepares us for our roles.

The apostle Paul affirms the unity of believers in Christ in remarkable passages such as Ephesians 2 and 3. He reminds his readers from people groups other than Jewish that at one time they were "strangers to the covenants of promise, having no hope and without God in the world." He affirms their position as "fellow citizens with the saints," as those living stones "being built together into a dwelling place of God in the Spirit" (Ephesians 2:11–22).

Paul then says that this melding of all believers into one Body had been a mystery "which in other generations was not made known to the sons of men, as it has now been revealed. . . ." Then he spells out that mystery: "To be specific, that the Gentiles are fellow heirs and fellow members of the body, and fellow partakers of the promise . . . in order that the manifold wisdom of God might now be made known through the church to the rulers and the authorities in the heavenly places. This was in accordance with the eternal purpose that He carried out in Christ Jesus our Lord" (Ephesians 3:5–11).

Now, the Jews had known for 2,000 years that God's plan was to bless every people group on earth. That they often ignored their bottom-line responsibility doesn't prove they were ignorant of it. In the same way, New Testament believers can often thoroughly ignore the mandate of the Great Commission while being fully aware of it. That God would bless all peoples was not the mystery.

To the Israelites of old, the mystery was that this blessing would bring these "heathen" *ethne* into unity with His chosen people! God's chosen Hebrew-Jewish people would not only pass on His blessing but would have as fellow family members those from every people, tribe, tongue and nation who were saved by grace! This was uncomfortable news; this was a head-scratching mystery.

This unity of one Body, one Spirit, one hope, one Lord, one faith, one baptism and one God over all and in all the diverse peoples (Ephesians 4:4–6) is illustrated by the human body. Each body part has either a slightly or an obviously different function; as Paul points out to the Corinthians, an eye is different from a foot. The various parts have varying abilities or "gifts"; an apostle (literally, a "sent one") fulfills a different function from a pastor. But the whole idea of the diverse body parts is so that the whole body functions, "fitted and held together . . . according to the proper working of each individual part" (v.16).

What is the Body of Christ doing? Going about His Father's business. Building the temple of living stones, which some day will be completed!

Remember that one of the parts of the Body referred to is those that are gifted as apostles or "sent ones." Just as we are not all noses in the Body, much to the consternation of some, we are not all "sent ones" in the specific sense. God equips some individuals to cross high, cultural barriers to proclaim His name; and this passage in Ephesians calls them "sent ones." We would call them "missionaries" today. We are not all missionaries, nor can we be.

We are all witnesses. But we are not all missionaries.

The job of the Body is to:

- Identify in our midst those who are designed by God to be cross-cultural workers or missionaries. Not everyone is a missionary any more than everyone is a pastor.
- Equip those sent ones with training.
- Send them out and support them.

So in terms of the front lines of God's battle to restore His Kingship over the earth, to offer redemption to the people groups of mankind, we members of Christ's Body are either sent ones or senders.

In World War II, it was estimated that behind every American combat soldier, fifteen support personnel made sure he was equipped and cared for. In the 90's, the ratio of support personnel in uniform to an American combat soldier is 20 to one. As we'll see, this decade needs to raise up nearly 100,000 new missionaries to finish the task of blessing every remaining people group with the Gospel. And if that is true, we meanwhile need to raise up perhaps 20 times that number of senders—those who are willing to join the Cause in sacrificial prayer and action behind the lines.

To keep the Body growing in unity as it incorporates more and more members from every people and tongue, the world needs two million vigorous, knowledgeable, equipped and effective senders to finish the task!

Are you a sent one? Can you use your abilities and gifts cross-culturally?

Are you a sender? Can you use your abilities and gifts in backup support of a sent one?

You're either one or the other.

And whatever your gifts, whatever your function in the Body, your role is critical in what the whole Body is doing. Even if you're peeling potatoes far from the front lines, your part is essential as the whole Body works together, being blessed to bless every people group.

The End

Obviously, there are other New Testament references and key passages we could study together to fine-tune our vision of God's unchangeable purpose. For example, Hebrews 6:11–19, the amazing New Testament commentary on God's sworn promise to bless Abraham and all the nations:

> When God made the promise to Abraham . . . He swore by Himself, saying "I will surely bless you, and I will surely multiply you." . . . In the same way God, desiring even more to show to the heirs of the promise the unchangeableness of His purpose, interposed with an oath, in order that by two unchangeable things [to bless Abraham and through him to bless every people] in which it is impossible for God to lie, we may have strong encouragement. . . . This hope we have as an anchor of the soul, a hope both sure and steadfast. (Hebrews 6:13–19)

Be encouraged to study through the many familiar passages of the Gospels, the history of Acts and the Epistles in light of the unchangeable purpose of God. New Testament Scripture reveals much more than the shortsighted details of the individual Christian life.

And be encouraged by the fact that there is an end to the story. Jesus said simply, "And this gospel of the kingdom shall be preached in the whole world for a witness to all the nations, and then the end shall come" (Matthew 24:14).

Regardless of your eschatology, your understanding of prophecy, the end of the Story of the Bible records the fact that the apostle John saw the finale of God's global plan:

> And they sang a new song, saying, "Worthy art Thou to take the book, and to break its seals; for Thou wast slain and didst purchase for God with Thy blood men from every tribe and tongue and people and nation. And Thou hast made them to be a kingdom and priests to our God!" (Revelation 5:9, 10)

The New Testament confirms the depth of God's heart for the whole world. It reveals the central point of history in which God as Man offers himself as the Sacrifice. And the New Testament clarifies the task: God is reaching mankind people group by people group, and there will be an end to that process.

For nearly 2,000 years since the close of New Testament events, God has been inexorably accomplishing His unchangeable purpose. In quiet, but amazing ways, God has been redeeming men and women in groups such as the Yao. And in astounding ways in global history, He has been reclaiming His territory among the peoples.

*P*ut on your traveling gear; we're heading south from Tanzania to one of the most beautiful places on earth—South Africa—and into its raging social unrest where the church is growing feverish with a vision for the world!

For Further Thought

1. List the New Testament references mentioned in this chapter. Then review each one as a follow-up sprint through the New Testament.
2. Find Tanzania on a map of Africa. Check with your mission agency to find out whether it has any work going on near this area, and ask if the Yao are targeted for church-planting. If so, pass on the news of the opening story of this chapter; such anecdotes can sometimes provide exciting keys to reaching a people group, such as the Yao, that may be settled in other areas.
3. Pray for the missionary profiled in this chapter's opening story. His name has been changed for security reasons, but he is a real person whose involvement in this true story is allowing him great windows of opportunity in his ministry to Muslims. Pray for Sheik Abu Bakr of the Yao that his incredible introduction to Jesus Christ will not be a source of pride but of great effectiveness in bringing Muslims to Christ!
4. Share this chapter's opening story as a source of "strong encouragement, sure and steadfast" with another believer who needs to be reminded that God is on the throne, and He is accomplishing His perfect purpose in every detail of all our lives.

VISION 2000

CHAPTER 9

The History of the World—Take Two! God's Purpose Through the Ages

*D*espite your media-inspired fears of bloody street battles and racial turmoil, you're strolling arm in arm with about a thousand young people—blacks and whites and coloreds and every shade of skin in between—on the main street of Wellington, South Africa. You're about 50 miles from Cape Town among the picturesque Boland Mountains, happy to be part of something that never hits the secular news: another "Bless the Nations" conference!

Marching in groups of 50, you're holding up traffic, singing and smiling in spite of the cool, overcast July weather. Workers lean out of their storefront offices to wave. Shoppers stare, dumbfounded. You sing "The Battle Belongs to the Lord" as you march past a park where the old men playing checkers scarcely notice your signs that read "Bless the Nations!"

The route of your march is down the same main street where more than a hundred years ago wagons rumbled over the cobblestones to carry missionaries into the heart of Africa.

You can scarcely contain your joy at finding in the political and racial pain of this country such a stirring, young-hearted revival. And it's focused on reaching out to the nations!

Just this morning, you recited along with the hundreds of students and their older church leadership what will be known as *The Wellington Call*. You shouted with the South African church:

> The God of Abraham, Isaac and Jacob, as in Exodus chapter three, verse fifteen, has spoken to us as He has formerly done in Covenant with our fathers, to the prophets, disciples and saints of

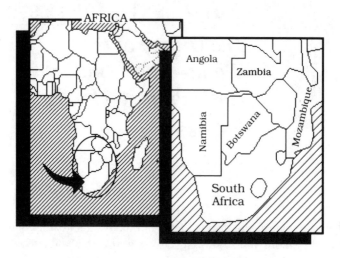

all ages down to the present. Now, through His Word, by prayer and proclamation, God has said we are to act with urgency and sacrifice to bless the nations to the glory of God with the Good News of salvation.

We are repentant, and soberly ask forgiveness for our attitudes toward other race and language groups, fully understanding that God does not allow such attitudes in the lives of His covenant-keeping children. We acknowledge that these sins have seriously hindered and limited prayer and missionary service both locally and beyond our borders.

We accept the fact that the Body of Christ in South Africa, as is the case anywhere, is made up of those called out and redeemed, made new and born again through faith in Jesus Christ, from all races, tribes, tongues and nations. We resolve to do nothing that harms this God-given unity, and also to take steps necessary for this unity, especially in missionary service to the unreached peoples in the years leading up to A.D. 2000.

We are willing to accept special responsibility, here in southern Africa, for certain unreached people groups, some of whom are our close neighbors, that we might send them missionaries, by faith, as a permanent obligation until they have their own Christ-centered churches and leadership.

You almost skip, arm-in-arm with believers of different races and different ages down the Wellington street. You can't help but think of God's promise to bless all peoples, to bring individuals together from all peoples, tribes and tongues into one Body:

> You were . . . separate from Christ, excluded from the commonwealth of Israel, and strangers to the covenants of promise, having no hope and without God in the world. . . .
> For He Himself is our peace, who made both groups [Jews and non-Jews alike] into one and broke down the barrier of the dividing wall . . . for through Him we both have our access in one Spirit to the Father.
> So then you are no longer strangers and aliens, but you are fellow citizens with the saints, and are of God's household . . . Christ Jesus Himself being the chief corner stone in whom the whole building, being fitted together is growing into a holy temple in the Lord. (Ephesians 2:11–21)

Laughing together as one Body in the South Africa drizzle, God's historic plan suddenly seems so obvious. How could anyone miss so many clear clues throughout the Word as to what He is doing to complete His age-old plan? How on earth did those lucky disciples who spent three years with the Word himself miss so many clues to the fact that He was a Messiah for all peoples?—That the point of God's purpose is clearly to offer His blessing of salvation in Jerusalem, Judea, Samaria and to every people in the uttermost parts of the earth!

Radical Worldviews

The Roman Diognetes received the following report from an outpost in the empire in A.D. 150:

> The Christians are distinguished from other men neither by country nor language nor the customs which they observe. For they neither inhabit cities of their own nor employ a peculiar form of speech nor lead a life which is marked out by a singularity. . . . They dwell in their own countries, but simply as sojourners. As citizens, they share in all things with others and yet endure all things as if foreigners.
> Every foreign land is to them as their native country, and the land of their birth as a land of strangers. . . . They are in the flesh, but they do not live after the flesh. They pass their days on earth,

but they are citizens of heaven. They obey the prescribed laws of the land and at the same time surpass the laws by their lives.

They love all men and are persecuted by all. . . . They are poor yet make many rich. . . . To sum up in a word: What the soul is in the body, that is a Christian in the world.

Fulfilling their role as salt and light, voluntarily or otherwise, Christians through the ages have spread the blessing of the redemption of Christ across geographical and cultural boundaries. Since nowhere in most of our educational backgrounds is there any systematic charting of this progress of God's blessing through the centuries, let's take the time to look back.

Let's catch the cosmic significance of our point in history.

From Abraham to the Cross

About 2,000 years elapsed from the time God changed Abram's name to Abraham, the "father of many nations," until the time of Christ. This span can be studied in five eras, each about 400 years in duration:

1. *The Patriarchal Period*

In roughly 400 years Abraham, Isaac and Jacob and his family succeed and fail at various times to pass on the blessing.

2. *The Period of the Captivity*

The possible ministry of the Hebrews to their Egyptian taskmasters for a period of about 400 years is seen in the tomb of one of the Pharaohs of the time. Inscribed in his tomb is a hint that he had converted to a monotheistic religion, and written there are several phrases of Hebrew songs that later were incorporated into the Psalms. Generally, we have to conclude that the Egyptian empire rejected God's offer of blessing.

3. *The Period of the Judges*

Told they were to function as a nation of priests (Exodus 19:5, 6), the children of Israel settle in a land most central to the world's trade routes. They begin to obey God's commands to rid their promised land of those nations that had come to their "fullness of evil," that had rejected the light of revelation. As a kingdom of priests, however, Israel itself degenerates into a helter-skelter mob in which "everyone does that which was right in his own eyes" (Judges 21:25).

4. *The Period of the Kings*

In the next 400-year period, God's redemptive purpose is more clearly defined as Israel's kings influence the peoples of the world in the name of the Lord God. The zenith of Israel's glory under the rule of Solomon is also the turning point of Israel's success in proclaiming abroad the excellencies of His name. The world first hears of young Solomon's fame because of the living God. Then the world hears of old Solomon's fall into idolatry, and God's reputation is defamed. A splitting of the kingdom finally results in captivity for both the northern kingdom and Judah.

5. *The Period Following the Exile*

In the roughly 400-year period between the end of the Jews' captivity and the birth of Christ, God's people learn probably more clearly than they have in centuries that God purposed for them to bless every nation. About a hundred years before Christ, a biblical, devout group known as the Pharisees begin to spread God's name in earnest.

Nearly two-thirds of the captive Jews stay in Iran or Persia, and their outreach efforts are considerable. Pharisaical missionaries push north until in every city, Moses is preached. As Judaism spreads south, Greek-speaking Egyptian proselytes and God-fearers help produce the Septuagint, the Greek translation of Scripture used as the Bible of the early church, and from which are taken 80% of the quotations of the Old Testament found in the New Testament.

Unfortunately, as these Jews "traverse land and sea to make a single proselyte," they begin to preach not so much the blessing of spiritual sonship, as an outward, cultural conversion to Judaism.

The Midpoint of History

Christ's birth, ministry, death, and resurrection are central to all of history. And as we've seen, Jesus comes as a Messiah for all peoples— to the Jew first and also to the gentile.

Five 400-year eras follow:

6. *The Roman Period* (A.D. *1 to 400*)

From the time of Christ to about A.D. 400, God's blessing slowly invades the Roman Empire. The message of a Baby being born in a stable spreads across about three centuries until Constantine, the ruler of the Roman Empire, moves his headquarters east into Greek territory to surrender the rule of his Roman palace to the leaders of the Christian movement.

So the seat of Christian influence moves to Rome, resulting in the translation of the Bible into Latin—the language of the western half of the empire—and the collation of the New Testament documents. However, the Romans did not pass on the blessing that had been brought to them.

As a result of their "blessing-hoarding," God sends the Gothic tribal peoples into the heart of the civilization of Rome to get what they were not sent: the blessing of the Abrahamic Covenant. They already knew of the Gospel, because earlier Rome had continuously exiled its Christian heretics into the northern and western parts of the continent.

7. *The Gothic, Celtic Period* (A.D. *400 to 800)*

The Gothic tribesmen and other European tribes such as the Celtic peoples not only receive the Gospel but produce beautifully decorated or "illuminated" manuscripts of the Bible to impress neighboring tribal chieftains.

8. *The Viking Period* (A.D. *800 to 1200)*

The Viking peoples to the north are the next to take what they have been denied. Their terrible raids on the Goths and Celts wreak massive destruction, but some of the young women they capture as slaves and wives are the messengers of the blessing of the Covenant! Over a span of 250 years, these ruthless peoples are gradually "held and dazzled by the effulgence of the glory of the Gospel," as Winston Churchill states in his *History of the English Speaking Peoples*. Overwhelmed as it were with the Gospel, they become Christian leaders of a sort in the next period.

9. *The European Period* (A.D. *1200 to 1600)*

These former ruthless pirates now lead ruthless Crusades against the Muslims in a pathetic misunderstanding of the Great Commission. Most of Europe's famous cathedrals begin to be built during a fifty-year period in this era, with the intention of glorifying God, and of out-doing each other! Bible study centers earlier established by Celtic missionaries and destroyed by the Vikings are transformed by Viking descendants into larger centers of order and worship. Some of these, with a particular emphasis on scholarship and education, become the first universities.

Also, despite the atrocities of the Crusades, missionary enterprise sees a new rush as strategists such as Prince Henry the Navigator and Christopher Columbus—both of whom are fired by devotion to Christ and to global missionary endeavor—search out new lands and new peoples.

10. *The Ends of the Earth* (A.D. *1600 to 2000)*
The period in which we find ourselves rivals all others in the extension of the Gospel. Let's look at it a little more closely.

The "End of the Earth" Era and God's Purpose

For nearly 200 years after the Reformation, believers, as is our pattern, focus on the top-line of the covenant. They study, analyze and notate the scriptural doctrines of our justification, sanctification, and glorification in Christ. The bottom-line responsibility that this blessing of salvation in Christ carries is largely left to a few zealous groups.

Great exploits occur during the 1500's, 1600's, and 1700's with the justification of "Christianizing" the world. Churches are planted in the Americas, on the fringes of Africa south of the Sahara, across the northern reaches of Asia, and in much of southern and eastern Asia and its bordering islands. In the secularized history that has been handed down to us, most of these mission enterprises are ridiculed for their imperialistic designs and cultural abuse of the heathen, noble native. A more realistic look reveals that much of this expansion does uplift the name of God among the heathen people groups of the world. For example, no secular history seems to bother examining the incredible ministry of the Danish-Halle Mission.

In 1705 the king of Denmark sends a team of German Lutheran missionaries to his colony of Tranquebar on the southeast coast of India. Of course you've never heard of Bartholomew Ziegenbalg, the godly missionary who stresses the need to study Hindu philosophy and culture to contextualize the team's church-planting efforts. He emphasizes worship—including Tamil lyrics, preaching, education, translation work, literature in the language of the people, and medical work.

And few secular historians know of the remarkable self-supporting work of the Moravian Church missionaries under the leadership of Count Zinzendorf beginning in 1734. Purposely sent to the neglected and despised peoples of the world, the Moravians are known for their cultural sensitivity and social interaction with unreached peoples as they patiently proclaim the Gospel.

A few more experts on the history of Western civilization do take note of a wrong-side-of-the-tracks young man who in the 1790's launched a mission movement of such magnitude that his bicentennial birthdate is being celebrated worldwide during the 1990's!

The First Modern Mission Era (1800–1910)—The Coastlands

As a young man, William Carey gets into trouble when he begins to take the Great Commission seriously. When in the 1790's he has the opportunity to address a group of ministers, he challenges them to give a reason why the Great Commission does not apply to them. They rebuke him, saying, "When God chooses to win the heathen, He will do it without your help or ours." He is unable to speak again on the subject, so he patiently writes his analysis, *An Enquiry Into the Obligations of Christians to Use Means for the Conversion of the Heathens.*

With a title like that his friends are impressed enough to create a tiny mission agency, the "means" for reaching the unreached. The structure is flimsy and weak, providing only the minimal backing he needs to go to India. However, the impact of his example reverberates throughout the English-speaking world, and his little book becomes the Magna Carta of the Protestant mission movement. Messengers are sent from Europe and America to spread God's blessing to the coastlands of the earth.

Carey's heart is best seen in the covenant repeated three times yearly by those working at his mission at Serampore, India. It remains a model of Christian enterprise to this day:

1. To set an infinite value on men's souls.
2. To acquaint ourselves with the snares that hold the minds of people.
3. To abstain from whatever deepens India's prejudice against the Gospel.
4. To watch for every chance of doing the people good.
5. To preach Christ crucified as the grand means of conversions.
6. To esteem and treat the Indians always as our equals.
7. To guard and build up the hosts that may be gathered.

8. To cultivate their spiritual gifts, ever pressing upon them their missionary obligation since only Indians can win India for Christ.
9. To labor increasingly in biblical translation.
10. To be instant in the nurture of personal religion.
11. To give ourselves without reserve to the Cause, not counting even the clothes we wear our own.

Carey's great watchword is: "Expect great things from God; attempt great things for God!"

His little book, in combination with the evangelical Awakening in America in the early 1800's, quickens vision and changes lives on both sides of the Atlantic.

In America, five college students, aroused by Carey's book, meet to pray for God's direction for their lives. This unobtrusive prayer meeting, later known as the "Haystack Prayer Meeting," results in an American "means"—the American Board of Commissioners for Foreign Missions. Even more important, their example starts a student mission movement that becomes the forerunner of other student movements in missions to this day.

Carey's influence leads some women in Boston to form women's missionary prayer groups, a trend that leads to women becoming the main custodians of mission knowledge and motivation. After some years, women begin to go to the field as single missionaries. Finally, by 1865, unmarried American women establish women's mission boards that, like Roman Catholic women's orders, only send out single women as missionaries and are run entirely by single women at home.

In the First Era of modern missions, progress on the field is painfully, agonizingly slow. Missionary after missionary succumbs to fever, especially in West Africa. Early missionaries are well aware that they are probably going to their death. Out of 35 who go to Ghana between 1835 and 1870, only two live more than two years. Yet the Gospel takes root and grows.

Where the Gospel goes to the coastlands of the world, the results are often amazing. As a result, in 1865, missionaries from the Hawaiian Islands (one of the earliest fields) begin to go home. They believe the job is done. With their withdrawal, the First Era in missions begins to decline. But another is about to begin.

122

The Second Modern Mission Era (1865–1980)—The Inland Frontiers

Hudson Taylor, also a young man, is considered impertinent because he tries to start a new mission organization. With much trepidation he does so in 1865, even though that's the year missionaries are being brought home from Hawaii. It takes 20 years for other missions to begin to join Taylor in his special emphasis—the untouched, inland frontiers.

One reason the Second Era begins slowly is that many people are confused. On the one hand, missionaries are coming home: "Isn't the job done?" On the other hand, there are millions and millions of unsaved individuals: "It's hopeless to open new fields!" There are already many missions in existence. Why more? Yet as Taylor points out, all existing agencies are confined. "Why go to the interior if you haven't finished the job on the coast?"

Finally, in the late 1880's existing agencies begin to retool for new fields, and a rash of new mission agencies are born with the new inland emphasis: the Sudan Interior Mission, African Inland Mission, Regions Beyond Missionary Union and others.

As in the early stage of the First Era, as things begin to move, God brings forth a student movement. This one is more massive than before—the Student Volunteer Movement for Foreign Missions. In the 1880's and 1890's there are only about three percent as many college students as in the 1990's, but the Student Volunteer Movement nets 100,000 volunteers who give their lives to missions. Of these, 20,000 actually go overseas. The other 80,000 stay home as senders.

By 1925, the largest mission movement in history is in full swing. Second Era missionaries have planted churches in 1,000 new places, mainly "inland." By the 1940's, the strength of these churches leads both national leaders and missionaries to assume that all additional frontiers could simply be mopped up by the ordinary evangelism of the churches scattered throughout the world. More and more people wonder if, in fact, missionaries aren't needed. Once more, as in 1865, it seems logical to send missionaries home from many areas of the world.

In 1967, the total number of career missionaries from America begins to decline. Why? Christians have been led to believe that all necessary beachheads have been established. By 1967, over 90% of all missionaries from North America are working with strong national churches that have been in existence for some time.

The facts, however, are not that simple. Unnoticed by most everyone, another era in missions has begun.

The Third Modern Mission Era (1935–   )—To the Ends of the Earth

This era is begun by two other young men, both Student Volunteers of the Second Era: W. Cameron Townsend and Donald A. McGavran.

Cameron Townsend is in such a hurry to get to Central America that he doesn't bother to finish college. In Guatemala, as in all other mission fields, there is plenty for the missionary to do working with established national churches. But Townsend is alert enough to notice that the majority of the population does not speak Spanish. As he moves from village to village, trying to distribute Scriptures in the Spanish language, he begins to realize along with certain other missionaries that Spanish evangelism will never reach all the people of Guatemala. He is further convinced of this when an Indian asks him, "If your God is so smart, why can't he speak our language?"

In response, Townsend launches Wycliffe Bible Translators, dedicated to reaching these new frontiers, the overlooked pockets of tribal people groups.

At the very same time Townsend and his friends are struggling with the challenge of groups isolated by language, missionary Donald McGavran is beginning to see the seriousness of India's amazing social barriers.

Starting in the 1970's, others, often disciples of McGavran, begin to realize even more clearly just how many unreached peoples exist in our world. They point out that many of these pockets of peoples have been completely overlooked by missionaries and national churches alike. These groups are defined by ethnic or sociological traits to be people so different from the cultural traditions of any existing church that mission (rather than evangelism) strategies are necessary for the planting of indigenous churches among them. Which brings us up to today.[1]

A New World View

Perhaps the history reviewed here bumps against the way you've always looked at things. For instance, most Christians are dumbfounded to read the personal journals of Christopher Columbus, which reveal so clearly his heart of love for God and commitment to spread the Gospel.

---

[1]This section adapted from the brochure *Four Men, Three Eras* by Ralph D. Winter, William Carey Library. See Chapter 13 for ordering information.

Most Americans have read only the secular history of Columbus' exploits, which is what is taught in the public schools. And it is almost shocking to realize that since grade one we might have been fed something less than the whole story about such a pivotal man in the history of our culture.

And if you have not been a student of the Bible, you might be feeling something of the same shock from our Bible studies thus far: How could I have missed this almost monotonous repetition of God's unchangeable purpose for the nations, the peoples, the gentiles! Why haven't I seen before the importance of God's name being lifted up, of our role as priests? How can it be that even in familiar passages, the obvious themes of God's heart for every people group has been overlooked in my years of hearing and reading those portions in church or Bible classes!

If so, what you're feeling is the basic uneasiness of a shifting worldview. A "worldview" is simply the way we look at things. What we do, what we value, what we think is true and real. And perhaps your worldview so far in life has been tinted by American cultural Christianity, which emphasizes personal top-line blessing and de-emphasizes the reality of Satan's counter-kingdom.

Cultural professor Norman Geisler explains our worldviews as a pair of colored eyeglasses. Our worldviews color everything we look at. And since most of us have been wearing one set of glasses since birth as we grew up in a culture, it's pretty hard to set those glasses aside and suddenly pick up a different pair to look at the world.

- Greetings reflect worldviews. In America, people grab each other's hands and shake them. In Mexico they embrace. In most people groups in India, greeters put their hands together and bow slightly; they're thus able to greet many people at once and don't pass on germs by touching. And to say hello, the Siriano of South America simply spit on each other's chest!
- Americans sit and sleep on raised surfaces because their cultural glasses tell them that floors are dirty. To many oriental peoples, floors are clean; so they of course remove their shoes at the door, sit and sleep on mats on the floor. To a Korean or Japanese, having a guest wearing shoes walk onto the floor is like a guest in America stomping across the sofa or bed with his shoes on!
- Paul Hiebert, professor of anthropology at Fuller School of World Mission, tells the anecdote: A mixed-culture group was eating at

an Indian restaurant when one of the Americans asked, "Do Indians really eat with their fingers?" "Yes, we do," the Indian replied. "But we look at it differently. You see, we wash our hands carefully. And besides, they have never been in anyone else's mouth. But look at these spoons and forks. Think about how many other people have already had them inside their mouths!"

In Latin, English, Sanskrit, Greek and several other languages, one meaning for the word "to see" is "to know." That is, the way we look at life through our cultural worldview "glasses" is the way we know it to be.

This fact has all sorts of implications if you're a person ministering within another culture. But it also has implications if you've begun to catch a vision of God's heart—of what He has been doing throughout biblical and post-biblical history.

Cross-cultural workers know that a change of behavior doesn't change a person's heart, that imposing Western culture on a person has nothing to do with a changed worldview. "As [a person] thinks within himself, so he is. He says to you, 'Eat and drink!' but his heart is not with you" (Proverbs 23:7). Making a people into a capitalistic, well-clothed parody of Western civilization has never been God's design for blessing the nations with the Gospel. His blessing comes by giving them new hearts in Christ—new, true ways of looking at the world.

So we see that our lifestyle doesn't really change until our worldview changes. And until our worldview shifts from the status quo, we aren't ready for training in a cross-cultural ministry.

Plotting Your Worldview

Think through the simplified diagram on page 126. The core of our worldview is the way we think in our hearts about what is real. This reality is formed by what we've decided about questions such as:

- Who or what is in charge of life?
- What is this Person or this force doing?
- Where do I fit in?

Unfortunately, what's very real to a person might not be true. A life built on a false reality will always be off-center.

What we feel is real affects what we believe. What we believe affects

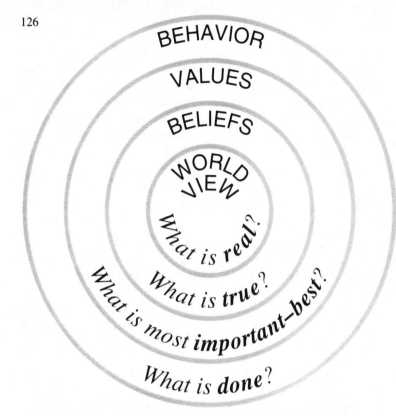

(Adapted from diagrams by Lloyd Kwast, Talbot Theological Seminary.)

our attitudes of what is good and best. And attitudes finally affect our behavior. Try to visualize the kind of worldview shift that might occur in your life as you catch the vision!

The typical American Christian worldview is something like this:

What is real? Well, God is real. He is basically on the throne, although a lot goes on in the world that He allows to happen because of man's evil choices. I fit into this scheme of things as His child who doesn't have a lot to say about cosmic events.

What do I believe? Among other things, I believe the Bible. I believe that God chose the Jews to finally bring forth the Messiah so He could start the Church so I could become a Christian—which means I'm different from the world, but if I live true to God I'll have a good life with His blessing. I also believe things are going from bad to worse, and when they get really out-of-hand, God will give up on humanity, Jesus will return, and I'll go to heaven.

What do I think is best? I think being a good Christian is extremely important—living a clean, godly life, reading the Bible, praying, witnessing, giving money to the church and missions and attending church services.

What is my behavior like? I try to do the things I know are important; but I don't do them as regularly as I should or would like to. I attend lots of meetings. And I'm basically trying to have the best life I can until Jesus comes back for me.

Now, this worldview may sound commendable, but is it based on what is true?

Let's look at a worldview based on the Scriptures we've studied:

What is real? God is minutely in charge of everything, even to the extent of using Satan and man's wrath to fit into His unchangeable purpose of blessing His people in order to bless every people on earth. I fit into a very specific role in that plan.

What do I believe? Among other things such as the doctrines of the faith, I believe God has been orchestrating His specific plan for all of history. I believe that everything that happens fits into His unchangeable purpose. And I believe there is a time coming when He will finish His plan. I believe that time is soon, and I believe my sense of vision of His plan is not a coincidence: I believe He wants to use me now in some significant way.

What do I think is best? Fitting into that plan. Seeking first His kingdom. Using all the disciplines of biblical Christianity to point in the direction of that purpose. It is important for me to maintain good health, cultivate good relationships, keep my finances in order so that I can give as much as possible to the Cause, walk in the paths of righteousness for His name's sake, and develop all my skills and spiritual gifts for my part in the big picture. I need to pray against the enemy strongholds so that God's kingdom can come on earth as it is in heaven, and pray that God would thrust forth laborers into His harvest. I must evangelize my own people group through personal evangelism, unite with other believers in this cosmic battle against satanic forces, and remain clean and pure as a vessel fit for God's use in His plans! All of this is extremely important because God is carrying out His purpose through us, His people!

What is my behavior like? It looks like typical Christian behavior, only a little more radical. I've never prayed so much in my life; I become angry over Satan's control over a certain unreached people group and I refuse through prayer to let Satan have his way over them. I'm getting together with Christians who mean business, because I know better than to tackle the strongholds of Satan by myself. I'm also studying the Bible and the world like never before, because I've realized how little I know about the whole picture. I spend a lot of time evaluating everything I do to pull it into captivity to obedience to Christ in His great Cause. I evaluate what I have and do according to the fact that it has a purpose far beyond making my own life comfortable. I find I don't do much in the way of trying to "keep up with the Joneses"; who cares about such small ambitions anymore? I'm feeling less of a need to escape; so I watch less TV and spend less money. I'm beginning to act as if I don't quite belong here in my old Western culture for much longer.

Think about it. Is *your* worldview ready to change?

*I*t's time to head to Europe in our armchair trip around the world. Time to nail down specifics as to where we are in the progress of the final task. Time to seek the Lord God of Abraham, Isaac and Jacob for our roles in His unchangeable purpose, in His plan that seems to be coming to a close in our era of history.

For Further Thought

1. Memorize Proverbs 23:7—"As a man thinks in his heart, so is he." Consider your own worldview. How would you fully answer:

   - Who or what is in charge of life?
   - What is this Person or this force doing?
   - Where do I fit in?

2. Give yourself a history exam. Review this chapter's sketch of global history. Then jot down each of the ten epochs of roughly 400 years each.

3. Carefully reread the "Wellington Call" and pray for the new mission movement in South Africa.

4. With a friend, discuss the inaccuracies/accuracies of the "typical American Christian worldview" and a "worldview based on Scripture." Explain to your friend the rationale behind each factor in the scriptural worldview.

CHAPTER 10

The Final Task:
It Can Be Done.
It Must Be Done!

*I*n Europe, the Church is not growing very impressively. The vision of God's heart for the nations is hardly a factor in the whirl of events and issues of the European Federation. But it is also the place where so many paths of so many peoples cross, you know you'll find more amazing evidence of God's global handiwork. Nearly every city in Europe is packed with refugees and other immigrants from hundreds of the world's unreached people groups—such as the Tajik from Central Asia.

You're in Utrecht in the Netherlands for "Mission!"—one of the world's most exciting gatherings of those increasing numbers of radical believers committed to discipling every nation. Thousands have gathered in this triennial mass of glowing young people from all over the Continent, just as in Urbana, Illinois nearly 19,000 gather every three years to assess who needs to go, who should send, and where we are in the great global conflict of establishing a church in every people group.

Last night you tossed and turned in your sleeping bag on the wood floor of a great hall along with about 2,000 others too excited to sleep. Today you met him—a shy, smiling young man of the Tajik people of Central Asia. You catch Ulmas's story as you sit over hot mugs of strong coffee in a cafeteria roaring with laughter, impromptu prayer sessions and talk. The story is relayed by three or four interpreters, all of whom are dressed in colorful pullovers and caps from Africa, the Middle East and Asia, and none of whom actually speak English or Tajik.

It was 1981, and Ulmas had been inducted into the Soviet Army

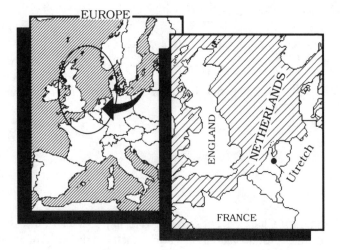

that was still occupying Afghanistan. His term as an orderly in a remote
Soviet Army Hospital on the border was just about over when a Russian
soldier gave him a Gospel of John. Many of the Soviet troops stationed
in Afghanistan during those days were Christians, sent to that dangerous
and demoralizing combat zone as "discipline" for their irritating religious convictions. God, of course, used these miserable assignments to
push His Gospel farther into Afghanistan than any missionary had ever
gone!

Ulmas was discharged, and as he rode a bumping bus day after day
along the mountainous roads toward home, he fell under deep convic-
tion of his sin. Pulling into his hometown and greeted gleefully by his
family, he found that night that he could not sleep. The words of this
Russian Book worried him, nudged against his staunchly Islamic worldview.

You excuse yourself to line up for another cup of coffee, and when
you return Ulmas is continuing his story to a gathering crowd, half of
which is wildly gesturing as they interpret into a dozen different languages for the other half.

You yourself don't know what to believe anymore after all the miraculous stories you've heard, but you listen spellbound as Ulmas says,
"I couldn't sleep because of the Book, so I walked through my town
until I came to the cemetery. Then I sat in despair. And suddenly it was

as if the Lord appeared to me! In blinding light!"

You remember hearing from several different, unconnected workers among Muslims that more than half of Islamic converts have received Christ after He has appeared to them in a dream! You lean forward to hear amid the babble of tongues.

Ulmas is saying, "He spoke very tenderly to me. He said He forgave me for my sin. Then He said, 'Feed my sheep.' "

And, as others of his Tajik group from the Soviet Union attest, he did just that. In spite of years of police interrogations and imprisonment, in the face of harassment from Muslim leaders in his town and region, Ulmas has been a faithful witness to the Lord's work in his life.

Just months ago, a Russian Baptist church in Tashkent invited Muslims to come hear more about Jesus, and, surprisingly, 400 openly filed into an auditorium. Traditional songs were sung; then Ulmas gave his testimony. When the auditorium fell quiet, Ulmas asked how many would like to receive forgiveness from Jesus Christ.

And every one of the 400 Muslims prayed aloud for "the forgiveness that Jesus gives."

Ulmas is hustled off by a few students in the crowd who are working in the Tashkent area, and you're left wondering about more details. One thing you're sure of: God can use Russian Scriptures handed out by Soviet occupational forces in bloody Afghanistan to reach Tajik Muslims for Christ. God is on the move.

Lessons for the Non-Missiologist

God has been pushing through the sweep of history to finish His clear, unchangeable purpose on earth: To bless His people so that every people may be blessed. And it's time we gear up more strategically to get in on His big plans for our own era.

To see where we are today in the outworking of God's overarching purpose, we need to review some basic concepts of reaching the unreached:

Politically

The common view is that the biblical term "nations" refers to countries. Political boundaries and geography are key in this outlook.

The accurate view is that "nations" refers to peoples. Cultural distinctions are key in this view.

Strategically

The common view is to focus on counting numbers of individuals who have come to Christ or who have not received Christ. This view often suggests that in order to complete the Great Commission we must spell out the Gospel to every individual on earth. Frankly, it's a pretty hopeless outlook! This view also uses the term "unreached people" to apply to any individuals who are not Christians.

The strategic view is to focus on potential movements toward Christ within people groups. People-group thinking forces us to consider whether a people group has a strong enough indigenous church movement to evangelize its own culture. If it doesn't—even if some individuals in that group are believers, even if Scripture has been translated into that language, even if there are some struggling, ineffective churches already planted—it is considered an unreached people. This strategic view accentuates the clarity of God's commission: The blessing of redemption is to be offered to every people; Jesus specifically commanded that we make disciples among every *ethne* or people—not of each person.

Culturally

The common view is that missions is anything done in the name of Christ at a distance from wherever we live. A missionary, then, is understood to be any Christian who is on a foreign, distant "field." In this view, geography again is the key.

The realistic cultural view is that the crossing of significant cultural barriers is missions. Preaching Christ within the same culture is actually evangelism. The term that describes crossing strong cultural barriers to plant a church among a people that has no indigenous church is frontier missions.

To sum up: We must think of the big picture of God's purpose on earth in terms of crossing cultural barriers in frontier mission to plant strong, evangelizing churches within unreached people groups.

The Final Frontiers

What is the remaining task? What is the status of the Great Commission in today's world?

- Roughly half of the world's population—actually about 3.05 billion—live in reached people groups. This does not mean all these individuals are Christians; it simply means they live in people groups where it's possible for them to respond to a clear presentation of the Gospel from within their own culture in their own language.

- There are about 13,000 reached people groups in the world.
- In the rest of the world, about 2.2 billion people live in unreached people groups.
- Currently there are probably about 11,000 unreached people groups.
- While about 900 of these unreached groups are scattered among various world cultures, 10,000 of them are primarily in five major cultural blocs:

    3,800 unreached Muslim groups. Nearly a billion individuals are Muslims.

    2,700 unreached tribal groups. Only about 140 million individuals are in these 2,700 groups.

    1,800 unreached Hindu groups comprise a population of

THE TARGET:

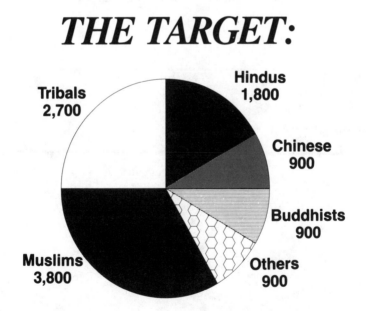

11,000 UNREACHED PEOPLES

about 550 million individuals.

900 unreached Han Chinese groups in which live 150 million individuals.

900 unreached Buddhist groups. About 275 million individuals are in these groups.

- These 11,000 groups in total are in 3,000 clusters which have similar cultural characteristics such as having dialects of the same basic language, etc.
- Most of the unreached groups are located geographically in what some scholars call "The 10/40 Window"—from West Africa across Asia between ten degrees latitude north of the equator to 40 degrees north.

Within this 10/40 window are:
- most of the world's unreached peoples (but not all, remember);
- two-thirds of the world's population, although only one-third of the earth's land area;
- the heart of the Islamic, Hindu and Buddhist religions;

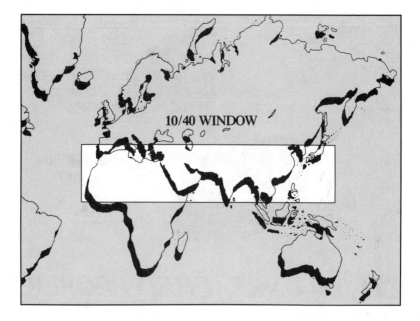

- eight out of ten of the poorest of the world's poor, enduring the world's lowest quality of living.

Mission statesman Luis Bush also points out that the 10/40 Window "is a stronghold of Satan." He writes in the *AD 2000 and Beyond* magazine[1], "As the Christian presence has expanded around the world, it appears that those people living in the 10/40 Window have suffered not only hunger and a low quality of life compared to the rest of humanity, but have also been kept from the transforming, life-giving community-changing power of the Gospel. . . . It appears that Satan has established a territorial stronghold with his forces to restrain the advance of the Gospel in this area."

Only 8% of the world's missionary force resides in this area of the world! Think through the following diagram:

Manpower isn't the only area of imbalance in our attempts to make disciples of every nation. The world's believers spend 0.09% of their income on ministries to non-Christians in reached people groups, where a church movement has already been planted.

But the world's Christians only spend 0.01% on reaching the remaining unreached people groups.[2] We won't, of course, dwell on where the other 99.9% of Christians' money goes!

Obviously, believers' efforts to follow Paul's example of going where Christ is not named (Romans 15:20) has somehow gone right over our heads!

Some people have suggested repositioning the world's 150,000 missionaries from working in reached fields to target unreached peoples. But the work being done among reached peoples is crucial too. Established churches in reached peoples need to be equipped, trained and motivated to not only evangelize their own people but to become sending bases to reach the unreached! Supporting the missionary workers and increasing our financing of this equipping ministry is definitely necessary to strengthen the new churches.

For example, God is strategically using North American cross-cultural workers among Latin American reached peoples. These workers train and equip Latins to share Christ within their cultures and to go out by the hundreds as new missionaries to the frontiers—particularly to the Muslims of North Africa and the Middle East.

---

[1]September 1990, p. 7.
[2]Statistics from *Our Globe and How to Reach It*, p. 25.

The Great Imbalance	Reached	Unreached
Individuals	3.0 billion 58%	2.2 billion 42%
People Groups	13,000 54%	11,000 46%
Mission Personnel	138,000 92%	12,000 8%

Source: Perspectives Study Program.

Shifting missionaries to target unreached peoples is not the answer.

Mobilizing the resources God has already provided and thinking strategically are the answers to the challenge of the remaining 11,000 unreached people groups of the world. Good news: The task can be done!

We Have the Resources

If in 1992 it was determined that there were just seven non-Christians for every evangelical believer, how much more encouraging the ratio must be today! (Look back at the diagram in Chapter 1, page 17.)

Now think through the ratio of Bible-believing congregations worldwide to unreached people groups:

What would happen if 500 churches banded together to become accountable for one unreached people group such as the Bozos of Mali? What could be accomplished if they together provided the prayer power needed, if they surveyed their memberships to put together an eight-person church-planting team, if they pooled resources to provide the home-support of finances and encouragement?

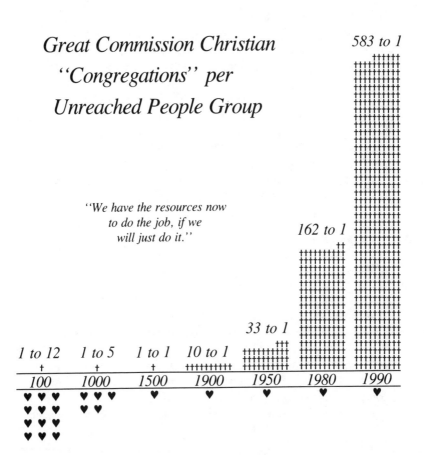

Great Commission Christian "Congregations" per Unreached People Group

"We have the resources now to do the job, if we will just do it."

What if just 100 churches committed themselves to reach one people group like the Bozos? What if just *ten* congregations determined to unite functionally enough to link up with a mission agency and reach that people? Or just three churches, or two? Or even one—your church!

It is not only possible to reach the Bozos and the 10,999 other unreached groups. It's possible to field those church-planting teams within just a few years! For instance, a personal appeal for help by the missionary to the Yao, whom we called Clarence Duncan, resulted in four missionaries arriving on the field within seven months!

Often the people of God will respond to a clear call; millions of dedicated believers in North America right now are restless to become a part of God's cosmic purpose—but don't know how! (In Chapter 12 we'll outline some clear specifics of what you and your church fellowship can do!)

We have the resources now to do the job, if we will just do it.

While we're working so hard to improve our lives, to deepen our fellowships, to seek God's healing of our families and our land, let's simply face the fact: We haven't yet discipled the 11,000 remaining unreached people groups as Christ commanded us.

Missiologists say that we can send church-planting teams into every one of these unreached groups within a seven-year period. To do it, we need:

- 100,000 new missionaries,
- to double our missions giving,
- more prayer—at least a collective hour per day for each new missionary.

God will accomplish His purpose. The gates of hell that lock in the unreached peoples of the world cannot stand against His Church. At the end of time Christ will be exalted with the song: "Thou . . . didst purchase for God with Thy blood men from every tribe and tongue and people and nation" (Revelation 5:9). Their being reached with this news is only a matter of when, and through whom!

Review the incredible amount of resources available to the world's 700 million committed believers. (See pages 87–89.)

The fact is that we have more than enough resources in America alone to complete the task:

- Of the 70 million evangelicals in America, 17.5 million are aged 18–35. The 100,000 new missionaries needed are only half of 1% of these young people available in the U.S.A. alone.
- American evangelicals have a disposable annual income of about $850 billion. About one-fifth of 1% of that income—$1.5 billion—would support the needed 11,000 church-planting teams.
- According to survey results, the prayer necessary would take only 2% of the time we evangelical Christians spend daily watching TV and shopping.

But this isn't a job for Americans alone. With 630 million other committed believers worldwide, the resources are obviously available. For example, it is estimated that by the year 2000 there will be 83,500 Asian missionaries on the job. In 1980, Korean churches vowed to send 10,000 new missionaries by A.D. 2000; but if they continue their growth rate of 725% per decade, they'll surpass that goal by 1995!

There are more than 2,000 plans operating right now that have as their goal the reaching of the entire world for Christ. Ninety-two of these plans are minutely detailed blueprints that specify how, with the resources we now have, every people, tribe, tongue and nation can have the opportunity to respond to the Gospel.

We can establish a church movement in every remaining unreached people group, and then help those new believers to evangelize their own people group. We *can* do it—if we *will*.

It Can Be Done. It Must Be Done!

Imagine. It's a September morning in 1913. We're standing on a rise over the ocean in a balmy tropical breeze. We're looking south to the white waves of the Pacific crunching onto the smooth sand of Panama. We turn and look back to the unbelievable sacrifice of years and lives and funds represented in the huge ditch carved through the ridges and jungles from the Caribbean 40 miles to the north. You remember how French engineer Ferdinand de Lesseps set out in 1872 to finish the task of a canal across the isthmus of Panama. More than 20,000 men died before de Lesseps gave up just seven years later.

225 Now you've extended what the French began, and you're within sight of completing the entire project. We're standing on a hundred-year-old chunk of rocks and dirt that still remains to be removed to complete the Panama Canal, one of the greatest engineering achievements in human history.

Chief engineer George Goethals strides up the slight rise and nods, "It's all here. We've got the dynamite to do it. The workers are ready. We've gone over the calculations again and again and figure we can cut our way through to the Pacific in about two days. We're ready. What do you say?"

As long as we're imagining, let's imagine you're the boss on this monumental project. What do you say?

When you see the end in sight on a huge project, it's not too tough to shout, "Let's finish the job!"

Now in the 1990's, the completion of the greatest project in history is within sight. It's determined that the Church has the necessary information, the necessary resources, and the necessary manpower to send church-planting teams to every remaining unreached people group on earth. The Edinburgh motto, "A Church for Every People by the Year 2000," isn't just a slogan anymore.

Blasting through the remaining tasks involved in this cosmic enterprise will not be easy; there will be blood, sweat, tears, and body counts. But, in the 1890's words of the evangelist D. L. Moody, "It can be done. It must be done!"

Many Hands, Light Work

Making disciples of every nation, of every ethne or people, is happening worldwide in two steps: mobilization and strategy.

Just as in wartime, when a country's entire population is mobilized in various roles, Christians on every continent are being challenged to find their strategic niche in God's global enterprise. Mobilizing the whole Church to its mission on earth is top priority to thousands of agencies and church associations worldwide. One of the foremost "generic" networks of these groups is called the AD2000 & Beyond Movement, headquartered in Colorado Springs, Colorado. Its slogan is "A Church for Every People and the Gospel for Every Person by the Year 2000." Some of the interest groups in the AD2000 & Beyond Movement coordinate efforts to mobilize prayer, to challenge youth, to enlist women in the global Cause, and to help local churches toward more hands-on involvement in world evangelization.

In various regions of the world, mission agencies are hoping to mobilize churches to take on their share of reaching unreached peoples. Although estimates are that more than half of the 11,000 unreached groups are already targeted, the task is clarified as the world's mission leaders announce accountability for a specific number.

Latin American evangelicals have committed to target 3,000—as proposed by Brazilian Edison Queiroz at the 1989 "Alcance 2000" conference in Costa Rica. Asian mission leaders at the Asian Mission Congress (AMC) in Seoul considered a plan in which Asian evangelicals would target another 3,000. AMC '90 Research Track Committee participants deemed it a "reasonable goal" that "all these peoples, by AD2000, have and continue to have opportunity to hear and understand the Gospel, and to receive and follow Christ in the fellowship of culturally relevant churches."

In North America, several mission organizations have suggested that evangelicals in the USA and Canada target 6,000 unreached peoples.

What these mission groups are hoping, of course, is that the churches in their regions will catch a vision of their part in propelling mission agency teams to the final frontiers.

On a country level, groups of evangelicals are implementing various mobilization efforts. For example, nearly 70 mission organizations in the United States are active in a growing "generic" campaign called The Adopt-A-People Challenge. Sweden, Norway, Denmark, the United Kingdom, India, South Korea, New Zealand, and Australia—so far—have announced similar plans.

Launched in early 1992, The Adopt-A-People Challenge urges those who want to mobilize their area for renewed mission vision to call 1–800-MISSION. Callers are given instructions on how to apply as a local task force coordinator, or how to link with an already-formed local team.

These interdenominational, grassroots, local task forces are challenging about 50 churches in their area to pray for a specific unreached people. Altogether, 300,000 evangelical churches are being challenged to adopt 6,000 unreached peoples for prayer and information-sharing.

Over a three- to four-month period, a task force typically:

1. Prays together for a revival of vision among area churches.
2. Drops off materials to each church leader to challenge that fellowship to pray for a specific unreached people. (For example, the churches of downtown Chicago are challenged to pray for the Berbers of Morocco; Albuquerque for the Turkmen of Central Asia; Seattle for the Uzbeks; etc.)
3. Organizes, so that long-term encouragement can be maintained for those churches adopting a people for prayer. Area concerts of prayer might be planned, the community newspaper's religion page might feature news on that people group, an area newsletter might provide prayer fuel, mission seminars and workshops could be offered to all churches, etc.

The local task forces in The Adopt-A-People Challenge are all linked by an electronic bulletin board. In each community, a local "computer whiz" is conscripted to connect by computer and modem to a national bulletin board. The Challenge BBS has news of global break-throughs among unreached peoples, tips for mobilizing churches in a community, prayer requests from missionaries on the field, announce-ments, fresh articles on what's happening globally, resources and op-portunities in mission work for individuals and fellowships, unreached peoples' profiles, and more. Local task forces are able, then, to share their successes and frustrations as they call believers in their part of America to a vision beyond themselves. God has put the technological gift of more than 50 million computers into the hands of believers around the world, and it's time that the Body of Christ link up electronically for His great purpose. (The Challenge BBS is handled by Logos-Online: 818/398–2428).

While believers are networking their mobilization efforts in their communities, resources are available to answer the basic question of "How do we adopt a people?" Many of these generic Adopt-A-People™ resources have been customized by denominations and church associ-ations to offer their churches resources that are geared specifically to their unreached people goals. For example, the Leader's Study Guide to *Catch the Vision 2000* (See Resources, p. 192) can be adapted with a mission agency's own applications, prayer requests, and action steps. (Adopt-A-People™ resources, and information on customizing them are available by phoning 1–800-MISSION.)

Some areas are reporting tremendous enthusiasm among churches. Other task forces are discouraged as very few fellowships respond to the challenge to pray that an unreached people be adopted into God's Family. But as results are tabulated and plotted on a map of the United States, it will become obvious whether or not the Church in America will respond to a clear call to forsake small ambitions, to integrate its ministries toward God's unchangeable purpose, and to rise to its destiny as a people who have been particularly blessed to be a blessing to every people!

After Mobilizing: Strategy

As a fellowship's heart is gripped to pray for an unreached people, it will want to become more informed, and more involved in actually reaching that group.

A congregation may "formally" link with a mission agency to reach a particular people. This formal adoption of an unreached people is a contracted commitment, and may involve raising up a team, providing funding, taking short-term trips—whatever that agency sets as its standards for formal adoption.

While mobilizing a church to its global role is a fairly straightforward process of catching a vision and building that vision through education and prayer, the strategy phase of the task is an exciting hodgepodge of all sorts of activities.

"Senders" in the local church identify "goers." Then they scurry around to provide support to those goers—moral support, prayer support, logistics support, communication support, financial support, and reentry support. (These roles are made practical in *Serving as Senders*; see Resources, page 192.) Researchers gather and sift through information from the field. Training facilities provide scriptural, cultural, relational, and practical education for missionary goers. And mission agencies try to tie it all together—keeping mobilizers in the churches informed, screening missionary candidates, forming teams, determining strategies and tactics, monitoring the work, and troubleshooting an operation that pits their goals diametrically against the entire world system.

Strategy is fast getting to be the most exciting phase of the mission of the Church as God blesses us with technological innovation and—particularly in the Two-Thirds World—with millions of potential harvesters. Many missionaries now communicate directly with their home offices by computer via satellite. The harvest force is beginning to look very nontraditional: Nonresident missionaries don't even live among the people they're reaching. The call is not so much for cross-cultural preachers as for businessmen and women, water reclamation experts, English teachers, producers of drama, computer programmers, tour guides, ethnomusicologists, etc. Most mission teams today are a multinational, multi-ethnic, multi-denominational mix of young and old, couples and singles.

Many of today's strategies to reach the unreached involve unprecedented cooperation among various mission organizations and churches. A Tagalog couple from the Philippines, for example, works under a mission agency from Singapore, is funded by an Indonesian church, and ministers in Paraguay! The largest Christian radio stations in the world have collaborated for several years in a joint effort called "World by 2000," in which they are complementing each others' programming so there is no duplication of effort. Their goal is that every major people group in the world will hear the Gospel in its own language by the year 2000. The eight world-level Bible societies have committed themselves to similar cooperation as they strategize to finish the translation of the Scriptures into every language, and to make that Scripture available to every person.

Both in mobilizing the Church, and in strategizing approaches, every step from prayer to action is multiplied as the Church works together, as every member of the Body of Christ does its assigned part. Every member of the Body, including you. You have a key role in the huge enterprise of being blessed to bless every people. Your part may be to:

- Strengthen the Church within the church for its *purpose*—to bless every people.
- Bless your own people group in evangelism, in standing up for righteousness "for His name's sake" among the nations, and in ministering blessing to the poor, to the oppressed, to everyone.
- Help the established church to evangelize its own culture, and to train itself as a mission sending base.
- Reach the world's unreached peoples.

In some specific way, you have a part in this vast enterprise. But you're not alone. As the last century's Student Volunteer Movement cried in their passion for the evangelization of the world, *"We can do it if we will."*

How many years will it take then to field teams in every *people group* within each cluster? To plant churches in each? To disciple those new believers into a strong enough church movement to evangelize their own people? In the words of an Authority: "It is not for you to know times or epochs which the Father has fixed by His own authority." All we need to know is that it is time to claim the available power promised through God's Spirit to witness in Jerusalem, Judea, Samaria, and to the remotest part of the earth.

We can plan. We can have church-planting teams in every people group within a few years—if we simply *will*. But it is God who orders our steps.

God is the One who has the real plans. He's orchestrating events in such rapid-fire sequence that we can't even keep up with the news of His exciting breakthroughs. Across the world, simple, isolated reports stream in—often from restricted-access countries among people groups where explicit publicity about Christianity would prove dangerous to

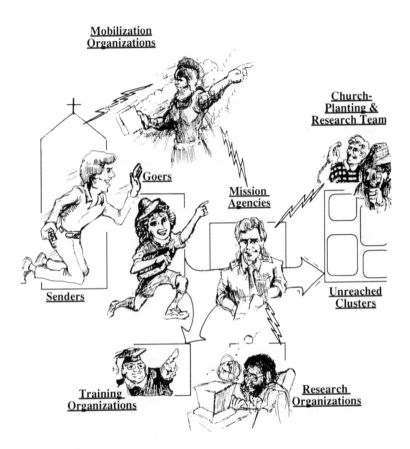

1. Clarify

2. Commit

3. Mobilize

4. Implement

the Christians there. Every year, thousands of remarkable, divine incidents never make it to the news desks for the front page or the six o'clock news. Most aren't even reported in mission magazines. Hundreds of breakthroughs to whole new people groups are represented by quiet, little-known stories such as the following:

> In an Islamic country, a Christian pastor had a dream in which he heard the words "Deegel, wa gese" over and over. The phrase means "Deegel, come and see."
>
> None of the pastor's congregation knew where Deegel was. So the dream was only a puzzle until six strangers arrived for a Sunday morning service. These weathered nomads made public confessions of their faith in the Lord Jesus Christ and said they were from a village called Deegel! They invited the believers to come and see their village.
>
> A missionary accompanied the pastor across the wilderness to Deegel, where the leaders of the group sat in the chief's hut and one by one said they wanted to follow the "Jesus Way." A gray-bearded old man claimed he had followed the Muslim path for more than 70 years, but, he said, God was now revealing to him and the people of his village their need of a Savior. Several of the men said they felt "their time had come" and they knew they must obey God.
>
> The pastor, missionary, and leaders of the village then prayed together. For the nomads, it was the first time they had ever prayed in their own language—since Islamic prayers must be offered in Arabic. The pastor and missionary assured them that the God of the stars would hear them in their own tongue, that He heard their heart-cries and was making himself real to them. The Deegel men nodded, "That is right."
>
> When the missionary offered grain in this time of drought, the new Deegel believers didn't want to accept assistance in case anyone would think they had become followers of Jesus just to get food from the Christians. As the pastor and missionary began to leave late that afternoon, the spokesman for the village insisted on walking with them to the nearest village to tell them about deciding to follow Jesus Christ.
>
> The name of the nearby village? Wa Gese—"come and see!" And why did the Deegel chief want the pastor and missionary to go to Wa Gese? Because they, too, wanted to follow the "Jesus Way!"(Adapted from Zwemer Institute newsletter 1990.)

The accumulation of simple reports like this one is overwhelming. God is doing things we can't keep up with. Our meager plans can't accommodate the pace of God's big-picture breakthroughs. He is doing something remarkable in our time.

Timing Is Everything

The last decade of a century is always marked by a surge of creativity, of drive. Any history buff of the West alone can trace in almost every discipline—from science to the fine arts to industry—a remarkable burst of accomplishments in the final decade of a century.

"More for emotional reasons than any logical cause," Marvin Cetron and Owen Davies of *Omni* magazine write, "The end of one century and the beginning of another is a time when creativity flows with special freedom. As the clock ticks its way through the tenth of ten decades and begins its next 100-year cycle, the themes that have shaped human affairs since the last great transition somehow seem to reach their zenith and conclusion, while the themes that will dominate the coming years begin to take shape."[3]

Even if the reason is only emotional or psychological, a sense of expectancy and drive will build in God's people throughout the world as we approach the end of the twentieth century. It makes sense, at least to our finite minds, that God would use this trend in His overall purpose. The year 2000 marks more than the end of a century—it marks the end of a millennium! For the first time, as a millennium comes to a close, the entire world is flipping the pages of the same calendar.

In 1951 when Mao Tse-tung took over as leader of the revolutionary People's Republic of China, the ancient rites signaling the new era were planned. In a time-honored ceremony, his followers gathered to honor the new dynasty with a new calendar beginning, again, with the year one. "Your Honor," they said, "what is the year?" And for the first time in thousands of years of Chinese history, the leader of the new "dynasty" replied, "the year is 1951!"

The whole world is on the wavelength of the Christian calendar. Every civilization on the globe is anticipating the close of this century and the beginning of the next millennium.

With a surge of global enterprise and creativity that surely will infect

---

[3]October 1989, "One Hundred Years of Attitude," p. 18.

believers, what can be done by the year 2000?

We're 4,000 years into God's promise to Abraham that all the people groups would be blessed, and the plan is intensifying. Hundreds of mission and evangelism groups worldwide have set A.D. 2000 as an arbitrary target date to finish the job of reaching into each people group. Note that this is not a time-limit for God to complete His work; rather it's a time-frame for us His workers to see what by the grace of God we can do!

At a 1980 world-level conference in Edinburgh, Scotland, 170 mission groups from 37 countries adopted the catch-phrase "A Church for Every People by the Year 2000." But if date-setting is forbidding to you, imagine it's 2041 and we can put a church-planting mission team within every unreached group within seven years. Would 2048 be a less threatening target date than 2000?

But why wait? Every day, more than 55,000 men, women and children die within unreached peoples that have never encountered the claims of Christ. These fellow humans beings are without God and without hope. Why should we wait to reach them?

Closure

God has put within the hearts of millions of His followers the hope of establishing a church for every people group by the year 2000. As U.S. Center for World Mission founder Ralph Winter puts it, "God expects us to do what is in our power to do, enabled by His grace. Anything that is possible for us to do is required!"

At the close of the last century, a distinguished group of visionaries collaborated to finish the task of the Great Commission. Stirring calls to prayer, to go and send were urged on hundreds of thousands of believers in America and England:

American pastor A. T. Pierson wrote,[4]

> In every generation a distinct and definite plan of Providence may be detected by the careful observer of God in history; and the true seers, the wisest and greatest in His eyes, are those who seek first to find out that plan and then fall into their place in it, and so serve their own generation by the will of God. . . .

[4]Quotes and following historical information from *Countdown to 1900*, Todd Johnson. New Hope Publishers, 1989.

These are days of giant enterprises in the interests of commerce, science, art and literature. Why not carry the spirit of sanctified enterprise into our religious life and work. . . ?

There is no lack of money nor means to compass the evangelization of the world within the present century if there were but the spirit of enterprise to dare and undertake for our Redeemer!

The leaders of the Student Volunteer Movement wrote in 1889:

Though in some generations the carrying out of such an enterprise might have seemed like a march up to the Red Sea with the command to cross, it is not so in this. Every door is wide open, all peoples can be reached, all mission boards are calling for more men!

But by 1895 it was obvious that unless there was a sudden, striking response from the Church, the task would not be completed by the year 1900. This distinguished group found themselves leading Western Christians into a Kadesh-Barnea experience (see Numbers 13–14). Would the 1890's believers challenged to the task believe it was possible? Or would they back away for fear of what such a grand enterprise would demand of them personally? The Israelites backed away from entering the promised land because of the obstacles reported by ten of the twelve spies. And 40 years later, their sons and daughters still worried that God would not use them miraculously to do what He promised to do. They had not learned the lesson of their ancestor Job: "I know that Thou canst do all things, and that no purpose of Thine can be thwarted" (Job 42:2). They hadn't learned from Abraham who, when God swore to accomplish His promise, "did not waver in unbelief" (Romans 4:20).

Advocates of finishing the task by 1900 challenged the Church to emulate the great enterprises of the past: Many at that time rehearsed how some 2,400 years before, King Ahasuerus of the Medes and Persians had translated, made copies, sent and proclaimed two very detailed messages to 127 regions from Eurasia to beyond India within one year. A famous anecdote went the rounds that a British army officer had been asked that if the queen of England were to give the order, how long would it take to reach the entire world with the Gospel message. After pondering the question, he simply replied, "Two years."

But every people was not offered the blessing of salvation in Christ by the year 1900. Toward the close of the last century, Bishop Thoburn of India wrote:

> A century hence, with a world so revolutionized by technology and the spread of the English language, the final conversion of all nations will no longer seem a far-off vision of a few enthusiasts, and the mention of a million converts will no longer startle timid or doubting Christians. We talk in hesitating tones about seeing a million converts now; but those who will fill our places a century hence will look out upon a scene where not a million converts but a million workers appear![5]

Are we bumbling into the same Kadesh-Barnea unbelief today?

When we learn of astonishing breakthroughs, will we in timidity and doubt think God can't sweep whole peoples to himself within a short time?

Just a few years away from its grisly reputation as an island of primitive headhunters, the country of Papua New Guinea recently announced that its national Law and Order Committee mandated Bible teaching in all the country's schools as an antidote to social problems.

Who during the dark history of communist rule in the Soviet Union could have predicted that a director of the dreaded KGB would meet on friendly terms with Christian journalists? Yet, following the breakup of the USSR and an attempted coup in 1991, such a meeting took place. Philip Yancy, editor of *Christianity Today*, recorded the KGB director's speech:

> "Meeting with you here tonight," Stolyarov began, "is a plot twist that could not have been conceived by the wildest fiction writer." Indeed. He then surprised us by saying, "How to bring peace and quiet to the hearts of people is a great problem for us. We are united with you in working together against the powers of evil."
>
> . . . Stolyarov continued, "We realize that too often we've been negligent in accepting those of the Christian faith. [The attempted coup of] August 1991 shows what can happen. But political questions cannot be decided until there is sincere repentance, a return to faith by the people. That is the cross I must bear. In the study of scientific atheism, there was the idea that religion divides people. Now we see the opposite: Love for God can only unite. Somehow we must learn to put together the missionary role—absolutely crit-

---

[5]Thoburn, J. M., *The Christless Nations* (New York: Hunt & Eaton, 1885).

ical for us now—and also learn from Marx that man can't appreciate life if he is hungry. . . . There can be no *perestroika* [democratic reform] apart from repentance. The time has come to repent of that past. We have broken the Ten Commandments, and for this we pay today."[6]

Books could be filled with similar events in the breakneck rush of God's moving to uplift His name among the nations. "Look among the nations," shouts the old prophet Habakkuk. "Observe! Be astonished! Wonder! Because *I* am doing something in your days—you would not believe if you were told" (Habakkuk 1:5).

Do we believe? Do we emphasize that a thousand years is to God as a day—so it may take a long, long time to finish the task? One curmudgeon grousing 100 years ago about the mission enthusiasm of his day said that based on his statistics, it would take between 300,000 to one million years to reach the world for Christ! Apparently he forgot the balance of God's equation on timing: A day is also as a thousand years. The enterprises of a millennium can be compacted by the God of the universe into just one day.

We now have resources such as transportation conveniences, sophisticated linguistic and anthropological training, computerization, video, fax machines, satellite communication, audio cassette players and recorders. Wycliffe Bible Translators are now able to do in days what before computerization took months; every 14 days a new translation of Scripture is begun somewhere in the world. Today there are more than 1,000 Third World mission agencies fielding nearly 40,000 missionaries where 100 years ago there were very few. Further, according to Ralph Winter of the U.S. Center for World Mission, "the facts are that it is roughly 20 times easier to complete the task this century than it was last century."[7]

We've seen that God's unchangeable purpose is clear. What isn't clear to many believers is the simple thought that this purpose will someday be fulfilled. Completed. Finished. The Great Commission was given in Genesis 12:2, 3 and Matthew 28:19, 20 to be *done*.

That simple concept was discussed recently at one of the most prestigious conferences of professors of mission in the world. As the group hammered out a new constitution, one of the participants suggested that

[6]*Christianity Today*, January 13, 1992, page 18.
[7]*Mission Frontiers*, June-October 1990, p. 45.

the term *missiology* be clearly defined in the new document. "How would you define it?" the group asked the participant.

"How about 'the study of the completion of the Great Commission'?"

The seminary and Bible college and Christian university mission professors looked at each other and said, "Completion? We don't teach that in our mission classes." And the suggestion was voted down.

But what about us, the non-missiologists of Christendom? Do we have any solid concept of God's global plan as something that had a beginning, that has been being played out for thousands of years, and that will be completed?

Jesus very simply said, "This Gospel of the kingdom shall be preached in the whole world for a witness to all the nations, and then the end shall come" (Matthew 24:14).

There will be an end. God knows when that will be. The apostle John has already seen in the future the fact that God will accomplish His plan to bring before the throne of the Lamb representatives from every people, tribe, tongue and nation (Revelation 5:9). And He knows whether we will do our part to hasten that day (see 2 Peter 3:12).

*I*f even in human terms it is possible to plant a church in each of the remaining 11,000 unreached people groups by the year 2000, is there any reason not to? As A. T. Pierson, last century's champion of closure, stated:

> This thought of a possible proclamation of the Word of Life . . . before this century closes . . . has never yet been shown to be either impossible or impracticable.

It can be done. It ought to be done. It must be done!

For Further Thought

1. Think through again and memorize the details of Matthew 28:18-20.
2. Plot out your own scenario of how your fellowship can help plant a church in an unreached people group. Actually diagram your scheme. Then, after some serious prayer, mark *your* place in that scenario. No manmade plan—yours included—is adequate for what God is doing, of course. But thinking through the steps will help

clarify your own strategic role in the general pattern of God's great purpose!

3. Spend a day this week in prayer and fasting on what God wants for you in the coming year, or how you can fine-tune your personal ministry within the Cause.

4. Bounce this chapter's "big plans" off a few friends. It's guaranteed to be a lively discussion! Although they may not have enough information to come up with an *intelligent* response, poll them on: "Is a church for every people by the year 2000 possible?"

CHAPTER 11

Warfare:
The Battle Belongs to the
Lord

*O*vernight you found yourself in blistering sunshine among crimson bougainvillaea blossoms and lilting Spanish. Bogota, Colombia is one of those global hot spots in the news with terrorist guerrilla activity, drug wars and assassinations. So, as you're learning, it's probably one of the hot spots of God's activity as He brings the offer of His blessing to every people. You know the Church is growing like never before throughout Central and South America. And you know that about 85% of the totally unreached peoples of Latin America are the Indian tribes in four countries: Guatemala, Ecuador, Bolivia and Peru. And Colombia is central to all four regions.

"You don't want to go there," your travel agent back in the U.S. had told you. "Nothing but trouble."

Since you flew in, you've seen nothing but happy kids skateboarding in the streets, yellow and red mosaic designs in the sidewalks and sunlight and flowers everywhere. Resting this evening in your world-class hotel room, it's hard to imagine Bogota as a hotbed of intrigue and violence.

But you know it's not far away.

It was just a few years ago that American missionary Chet Bitterman was killed by guerrillas. Just a few years since Bruce Olson was kidnapped by terrorists. And yet in the dark danger of the jungles and the people-packed, bright, cosmopolitan cities of Latin America, the beauty and the poverty, you know God has been carrying out His promise to every people.

But God's global push is not limited to South American jungle tribes. In fact, all of Latin America is buzzing with news of the growth

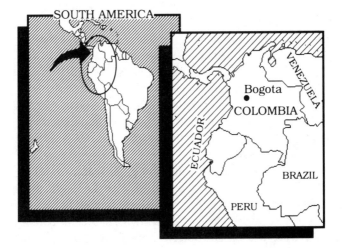

of the evangelical church and its growing status as a mission sending base.

Of the 400 million Latin Americans, more than 40 million have become evangelical Christians. Even secular, world-watching publications such as *World Press* observe that living Christianity is sweeping across the Latin world. "The [Roman Catholic] church's golden age is drawing to a close, and a quiet revolution comparable to the Reformation in 16th-century Europe is taking place."[1]

By the end of this decade, a majority of the people in Brazil, Guatemala, Honduras, and El Salvador will be evangelical believers. Chile, Costa Rica, and Bolivia will be about 40% Bible-believing evangelical. Already Mexico's population is more than 35% evangelical. São Paulo, Brazil, is home to one of the world's largest congregations with more than 20,000 members attending each week. One denomination in Brazil began 50 years ago with three North American missionaries; within the past five decades it has exploded into more than 8,000 churches.

Latin American churches are becoming solid sending bases. In Brazil, the Valley of Blessing mission school has sent out Brazilians to 30 different countries. Surinam and Nicaragua have trained and sent their

[1]*Der Spiegel*, March 1991, p. 30.

own missionaries to North Africa. Mexico and Honduras have hundreds of missionaries in the Middle East.

God is breaking through with head-shaking strategies in Latin America. You recall the missionary letter you left at home. It seems a year ago an American Wycliffe Bible Translators couple in Peru was attacked by a band of rebel guerrillas. The soldiers stole the couple's car, generator, and movie projector. After the rebels finally decided not to kill the couple and headed back into the jungle, the missionaries offered, "You might as well take the movies too." The rebels grabbed the film reels and disappeared.

This year the couple heard that Jorge, the leader of that group, was jailed in a nearby town. Steeling themselves to visit and forgive the man, they were shocked to find he claimed to have become a believer! The year before, at the rebel camp, the men had become bored. Thinking the Americans had been profiteering by showing Rambo movies, the guerrillas fired up the generator, popped on the film reels, and began watching a film based on the life of Jesus. They showed a full seven reruns of the movie in the rebel camp, and Jorge said that many of them laid down their arms to follow Jesus Christ!

God is working in miraculous ways, but there is plenty more to be done in Latin America. For example, the present-day Incas, the Quechuas of Ecuador and Peru, still worship the animist nature god of the sun. Dozens of tribes in the Amazon River basin who are struggling to survive in the violent lawlessness of the continent's final frontiers still live firmly in the clutches of the god of this world. But the bursting-at-the-seams evangelical church in Latin America is making inroads into every people group on the continent, even though the black magic of satanic power is evident everywhere.

Satan seems to get his tentacles around every group in which his usurped kingdom stands in jeopardy, where the possible light of the glorious Gospel of Christ might shine into the hearts of those enslaved in his darkness.

It's late-night in Bogota, and you realize your thoughts have been drifting, and you don't like their dark direction. You step over to your hotel room window and look out at the city which today was beautiful, sunny. Telling yourself it's because you're used to the blaze of big-city lights in the U.S.A., you feel uneasy at the blackness of the city.

And you remember that the exciting, global-scale push to bring the Gospel to every *ethne* isn't just a simple matter of reaching human beings. All the extraordinary plans to evangelize the world by A.D. 2000 are also up against the kingdom of darkness. The prince of this world is going to make sure the final task of completing the Great Commission will not be easy.

This is not a game.

The Catch

Through our study, you might have wondered: If the biblical mandate is so clear, if the big picture of what God is doing in our world today is so exciting, if the 11,000 remaining people groups could be reached within a few years' time, if millions are dying without God and without hope, if we can push back the powers of darkness over whole nations near to the heart of God, why isn't all Christendom buzzing with the news that we can finish the task? What's the catch?

Here's the easy answer: There is a cost involved.

That's the catch. Obedience costs. Real discipleship costs. The price? Giving up our small, personal agendas that detract from God's global Cause. Forsaking our comfortable lives, giving up claims of ownership to affluence, to security.

The challenge today is exactly that of Francis Xavier who 500 years ago dreamed of returning to Paris from his mission work in India, China and Japan. Why? So he could "go shouting up and down the streets to tell the students to give up their small ambitions and come eastward to preach the Gospel of Christ!"

The cost for Christian organizations is to give up small ambitions, to selflessly cooperate, not needlessly duplicate efforts and compete for funds. Paul McKaughan of the Evangelical Fellowship of Mission Agencies says to these organizations:

> It is important that we as leaders begin to interact together and find out what God's will is for us collectively. . . . We may be talking about surrendering some of our prerogatives. We may be talking about applying some of our computer skills. We may be talking about some of our unreached peoples ground forces.
>
> We are all accumulating a body of knowledge and we're all trying to do everything. We can't do everything in the world in which we live. And we're going to have to begin to trust one another enough to use the tools and the abilities and the giftedness of the various members of our community in order that the body of Christ

can move with an expeditious and a decided tread toward this goal of world evangelization.[2]

Obedience means giving up our small, personal ambitions. Obedience means shifting our expectations to becoming a blessing instead of merely being blessed. The price of being a part of God's historic, global purpose is losing your life for His sake. Denying your old self. Taking up your cross—which in Jesus' day meant you wouldn't need to worry much about things that most people worry about. Taking up your cross is a picture of your standing with a noose around your neck; you've put yourself at God's disposal so thoroughly that you have nothing left to lose.

An old parable often told among believers across Africa pictures just how tough it is to give up our own ambitions:

> One day Jesus asked each of His disciples to pick up a stone to carry for Him. John took the biggest one he could find, while Peter picked a small one. Jesus took them up to the top of a mountain and commanded the stones to be bread. Each was allowed to eat the bread he found in his hands, but of course Peter did not have much to eat at all. John then shared some of his with Peter.
>
> On another occasion Jesus again asked the disciples to carry stones for Him. This time, instead of leading them to a mountaintop, he took them to the River Jordan. "Cast the stones into the river," was His command this time. The disciples looked at one another in bewilderment. What could be the point? They had lugged those stones all this way (And you know who picked the big one this time, don't you?). Throw them into the river? Why? But they obeyed.
>
> Jesus turned to them and said, "For whom did you carry the stone?"

Sometimes the Christian disciplines of denial of self, of facing afflictions, of solid prayer and study in the Word seem pointless. What's the purpose of denying self and taking up your cross daily? A nicer life? Success? Or is discipleship a discipline with purpose: To become a closer follower of Christ, to live in obedience to "make disciples of all *ethne*."

Jesus didn't pander to our lazy, self-seeking instincts:

---

[2]"A.D. 2000 and Beyond," A.D. *2000*, May-August 1990, pp. 5–9.

He who loves father or mother more than Me is not worthy of Me; and he who loves son or daughter more than Me is not worthy of Me. And he who does not take his cross and follow after Me is not worthy of Me. He who has found his life shall lose it, and he who has lost his life for My sake shall find it. (Matthew 10:37–39)

And looking at him, Jesus felt a love for him, and said to him, "One thing you lack: go and sell all you possess, and give to the poor, and you shall have treasure in heaven; and come, follow Me." (Mark 10:21)

And another also said, "I will follow You, Lord; but first permit me to say good-bye to those at home." But Jesus said to him, "No one, after putting his hand to the plow and looking back, is fit for the kingdom of God." (Luke 9:61, 62)

So therefore, no one of you can be My disciple who does not give up all his own possessions. (Luke 14:33)

There are many fine expositions and Bible studies published on these and other "hard" passages concerning the disciplines of true discipleship. But even the most earnest attempts to soften these stringencies of following Jesus must conclude that the price of selling yourself as a bondslave for the Master's use can be high. In the Bible, a life sold out to His purpose is compared to the rigors of the lifestyle of an athlete in training, a hard-working farmer, a combat soldier (2 Timothy 2:3–10).

Can we visualize—can we ever forget—the fact that since the time of Christ, 40 million believers have been martyred for faith in Jesus Christ? In recent times, the total number of Christians killed for their faith is 300,000 every year!

Perhaps too many of us Christians have been led to believe that Christianity is supposed to be nice—respectable, predictable and smooth. We are deceived into thinking that being the people of God means lots of meetings and lots of blessings.

But God's big purpose for leaving you on this earth is not to put you through a spiritual health spa regimen to make you feel better. He'll do all that in heaven in the twinkling of an eye. Life on earth is war. And war is never nice.

God says that Satan's world system is out to get us (John 15:18, 19). He suggests that humans dedicated to the satanic counter-kingdom can destroy us. For example:

A king will arise
Insolent and skilled in intrigue.

And his power will be mighty, but not by his own power.
And he will destroy to an extraordinary degree
And prosper and perform his will;
He will destroy mighty men and the holy people. (Daniel 8:23, 24)

Why isn't all of Christendom humming with the excitement of finishing the task? Because it's not exactly going to be a breeze. Since it's global war, there are going to be casualties and body counts. Living out your part in God's great purpose won't be easy.

Prisoners in the Dungeon

South America is a continent that people by people, area by area is being released from the stranglehold of Satan's principalities, powers and rulers of darkness. This was the continent infested with Nazi war criminal fugitives following World War II; the site of the grisly mass suicide of nearly 900 followers of the cult leader Jim Jones in the 70's.

And it may be a good place to pause and visualize again the interwoven threads of God's twofold plan, one that incorporates the abolishing of Satan's counter-kingdom and at the same time the redemption of humans held captive in the bonds of darkness.

Imagine. You're in a Jim-Jones-style compound somewhere in the thick of the jungles of Bolivia. You help cultivate and harvest the crop of bananas, you live in a passable bungalow in the village, and your entire social structure is framed around others in the village and their allegiance to a Nazi cult leader. Perhaps it's just after the close of World War II and the signing of the pact that signaled the absolute, utter defeat of the Nazi government in Germany.

Your leader directs the basic activities in the village. You're frankly afraid of him, knowing his rumored background as a concentration camp murderer. You once witnessed his brute cruelty when a villager refused to work; the leader had rationed that man's food allotment, then had him beaten and thrown out of the compound into the jungle. The leader is unquestionably the boss around here. He makes sure the village has enough food, he officiates at all the social functions—the marrying and burying, and you simply go along with all the others in following his leadership. It's as if there isn't much choice.

You can continue the allegory, but the point is clear: An officially defeated despot can still rule over a group of people who allow him to rule over them.

Satan and his principalities and powers still rule over peoples who continue to invite him to be their ruler. He has been officially defeated—on the cross Christ "disarmed the rulers and authorities; He made a public display of them, having triumphed over them" (Colossians 2:15). But God's time plan still pinpoints a future date when Christ "delivers up the kingdom to the God and Father, when He has abolished all rule and all authority and power" (1 Corinthians 15:24). The die is cast: Satan as "the ruler of this world shall be cast out" (John 12:31).

In the meantime, Satan's diabolical world system is busy "deceiving the nations" (Revelation 20:3). Today about 12,000 people groups virtually believe they have no choice but to be subject to Satan's rule—whatever form that rule may take. The dark god of this world system has blinded their minds (2 Corinthians 4:4) so they as a people can't see the light of the Gospel even if it were beamed brilliantly from space!

Look back at the opening narrative in chapter two to remind yourself of the Naxi, the people who worship Yama, the god of death. How can the glorious light of the Gospel of Christ shine in the hearts of the Naxi? These people are captive to the principality or power that rules them.

And here we are as God's "royal priesthood . . . called . . . out of darkness into His marvelous light" (1 Peter 2:9). Isn't it only fair that we act in our priestly role as intercessors for the Naxi?

But then, taking up the cause of the Naxi is not going to be easy. Yama is not going to give up without a fight.

Soldier Priests

God says to His people,

I have called you in righteousness . . .
As a light to the nations [such as the Naxi],
To open blind eyes,
To bring out prisoners from the dungeon,
And those who dwell in darkness from the prison.
I am the Lord; that is My name. (Isaiah 42:6–8)

Jesus spoke of the principle that you can't "enter the strong man's house and carry off his property"—to rescue the perishing—"unless [you] first bind the strong man." The wording in the original Greek here emphasizes the article "the"; Jesus is referring to a particular strong man—Satan. Then, Jesus said, you can "plunder his house!"

(Matthew 12:29). Now, Satan and his organized hierarchy of principalities, powers and rulers of darkness are spiritual entities. They are creatures of "the heavenlies." How can we with our feet on the ground "bind the strong man" to bring out prisoners such as the Naxi from Satan's dungeon?

Christ entrusted to God's people the incredible priestly duty of agreeing together to bind and loose: "Whatever you shall bind on earth shall be bound in heaven; and whatever you loose on earth shall be loosed in heaven" (Matthew 18:18; see also Matthew 16:18, 19). Our struggle, Paul clearly insists, is not against humans—flesh and blood—but against the powers that manipulate them in Satan's world system: "Our struggle is . . . against the rulers, against the powers, against the world forces of this darkness, against the spiritual forces of wickedness in the heavenly places" (Ephesians 6:12).

What do we do in this struggle? "Though we walk in the flesh, we do not war according to the flesh, for the weapons of our warfare are not of the flesh, but divinely powerful for the destruction of fortresses" or strongholds—even if the structure of those strongholds is buttressed on nothing more tangible than world-system ideas: "speculations and every lofty thing raised up against the knowledge of God" (2 Corinthians 10:3–5). (The 70-year domination of millions under Communism should tell us what effect a satanically backed idea can have.)

Agreeing in prayer is, of course, a primary weapon:

- *Pray to pull down satanic fortresses over unreached people groups* (2 Corinthians 10:3, 4; see also "How to Pray for Unreached Peoples" in the Appendix). Go ahead, vent your anger in prayer against the powers of evil that hold 11,000 people groups under the cruel, ugly, destructive god of this world. It's not fair! Life under the domain of darkness is not just. Innocent people are caught in its trap. If we accept their condition as "just the way it is," we've given in to the world-system's status quo. Someone has suggested that prayer is the ultimate rebellion against the status quo. It's all right to be angry; refuse to accept the injustice, the horrible destitution, the preventable illnesses. And, as the poor widow persisted in presenting her case because of the injustice done her (Luke 18:1–8), persist in prayer until victories are won in the heavenlies.

  Even if you can't work up your own anger against Satan's

domain, take God's side in the matter. God's wrath against evil never cools. Intercede—refusing to accept the way things are in the world. That is the very nature of spiritual warfare in prayer.

- *Pray for the saints involved in reaching the captives.* Listen to Paul's clear plea for prayer that closes his warning to put on the whole armor of God:

> With all prayer and petition pray at all times in the Spirit, and with this in view, be on the alert with all perseverance and petition for all the saints, and pray on my behalf, that utterance may be given to me in the opening of my mouth, to make known with boldness the mystery of the gospel. (Ephesians 6:18, 19)

- *Pray for new laborers.* You've been looking at the fields that are ripened for harvest. Now "beseech the Lord of the harvest to send out workers into His harvest" (Matthew 9:38). Remember that the term for "send out" is more correctly translated "thrust out." It is the same word used when Jesus thrust out the moneychangers from the temple's court of the gentiles, the same New Testament term used for casting out spirits. Being "thrust out" may even be a bit uncomfortable for those God sends into His harvest. But pray!

Another weapon of our warfare in the heavenlies is a strong testimony—one that means business, that says we are willing to go to extremes in obedience to Christ. The blood-bought authority with which Christ directs His harvest of making disciples of all the nations (Matthew 28:18, 19) empowers our testimony to break the grip of Satan, "who deceives the whole world." John writes:

> And I heard a loud voice in heaven saying, "Now the salvation, and the power, and the kingdom of our God and the authority of His Christ have come, for the accuser of our brethren [the meaning of Satan's name] has been thrown down. . . . And they overcame him because of the blood of the Lamb and because of the word of their testimony, and they did not love their life even to death." (Revelation 12:10, 11)

Though a testimony may seem a vague weapon in spiritual warfare, accept it as fact: A surrendered life cleansed by the blood of Christ can break through Satan's barriers to bring light to the captives!

Another weapon used to defeat Satan's minions is a combination of faithful prayer and fasting; Christ said that some powerful spirits of the counter-kingdom don't give up their rulership "except by prayer and fasting" (see Matthew 17:14–21).

A more obvious weapon is the sword of the Spirit, which is the Word of God (Ephesians 6:17). It is an offensive weapon to be used against the forces of the evil one. Jesus used it skillfully in the incident recorded in Matthew 4:1–11. But it is important to note that abiding in the Word isn't just head knowledge of Scripture. No mere intellectual compilation of the Bible's information daunts Satan—he can quote Scripture too, and answer trivia questions about the Bible probably long before you can! The weapon that defeats the deception of the enemy is truth; and Christ said that the Word is truth (John 17:17). Let the Word of Christ *dwell* in you richly.

There are more weapons in our spiritual arsenal. But before you tackle serious spiritual battling for the sake of God's unchangeable purpose, be forewarned. Spiritual warfare is not a new fad in the American Christian culture; it is not a game.

Satan and his world-system organization are powerful. Perhaps you thought that spiritual warfare amounts to battling the awesome hordes of hell over your temptation to watch too much TV or eat an extra eclair. Fighting against our flesh, denying self is one thing. Warring against the satanic counter-kingdom in behalf of an unreached people group is more like going into battle with 10,000 soldiers against a king who has 20,000. Our meager resources are no match for his (see Luke 14:28–32). This diabolical army knows man's weaknesses; Satan's representatives can actually "wear down the saints of the Highest One" (Daniel 7:25).

Peter Wagner warns: "Dealing with territorial spirits is major league warfare and should not be undertaken casually. I know few who have the necessary expertise, and if you do not know what you are doing, Satan will eat you for breakfast."

He suggests two examples in the *Evangelical Missions Quarterly*:[3] Wilson Awasu, one of Wagner's students, reported that in Ghana a pastor, over the protests of his congregation, oversaw the cutting down of a tree that had been enshrined by satanists. As the last branch was sawed off, the pastor suddenly collapsed on the spot and died. As

---

[3]July 1989, p. 287.

another pastor demolished a fetish shrine, he inexplicably suffered a stroke. Wagner's advice? Never underestimate the power of the enemy.

Never underestimate the danger of battle. Paul wrote constantly of afflictions, hardships, hunger, beatings, and imprisonment. As God's people are gathered together into one from among the nations (John 11:52), as we make known "the riches of the glory of this mystery among the gentiles," we need to be aware that some individuals will be called upon to "fill up that which is lacking in Christ's afflictions" (Colossians 1:24–29). Paul urged that "no man may be disturbed by afflictions; for you yourselves know that we have been destined for this" (1 Thessalonians 3:3).

Paul knew the reality of the enemy. With the possible exception of the book of Philemon, all of Paul's writings refer to Satan and his plans to destroy believers' priestly ministry of grace and apostleship. God's command through Paul to "take up the full armor of God that you may be able to resist in the evil day" (Ephesians 6:13) suggests we need to be prepared for something a bit more dangerous than the monthly church potluck.

Is it any wonder that not too many of the 70 million evangelical believers in America are signing up to finish the task, to follow to the death God's clear mandate of discipling the nations?

Hell Hath Fury

Satan delights when believers cheat, lie, swear, swagger in drunkenness, hate each other, get jealous, and spread rumors, because their sin defames God's great name. But these sinful activities, shameful as they are, have little effect on the state of Satan's counter-kingdom. He can allow plenty more believers to attend church regularly, clean up their lives, and even pray for one anothers' illnesses. In fact, he can let a few Christians' relatives and neighbors come to Christ without worrying about his evil forces being thwarted in the least.

However, there is one thing Satan is ultimately concerned about: himself. He knows Scripture better than any believer, and he knows he will eventually be relegated with his demonic hordes to the Lake of Fire (Revelation 20:10). The only thing he can do meanwhile is to "buy time."

One major factor in Scripture spells out the timing of his final doom. So if there is a key biblical passage Satan is ultimately concerned about, it is a simple verse in the book of Matthew: (One mission thinker suggests that if there is a boardroom in hell, this is the verse inscribed over the podium.)

> And this Gospel of the kingdom shall be preached in the whole world for a witness to all the nations, and then the end shall come. (Matthew 24:14)

An end to Satan's reign is a personal threat to him. And regardless of your views on future events, this verse clearly equates the end with the proclamation of the Gospel as a witness to all the nations, to every people group on the face of the earth.

As we thrust forth laborers into the harvest, as we endure hardship as good soldiers for the Cause of Christ, as we gird ourselves to remain standing in spiritual battle, people group after people group will be reached. The countdown has begun. Satan's dominion over the peoples is, in the present progressive words of John, "passing away" (1 John 2:17).

The closer we get to that time when the last unreached people group will witness the proclamation of the Gospel in its own culture, in its own language, the closer Satan comes to the end.

And "knowing that he has only a short time," the devil rages (Revelation 12:12).

The final task of reaching every people on the face of the globe will not be painless. We have an adversary. But God is looking for a few good men and women to fight the good fight, to overcome. "He who has an ear, let him hear what the Spirit says to the churches" (Revelation 3:22).

Storming the Gates

So the battle of Christendom is to confirm God's claim on people group after people group, to pull down the satanic strongholds that keep them prisoners of darkness. It is a progressive war, with battles won and lost in the heavenlies—casualties, blood, sweat and tears on the ground. But the gates of hell will not stand against the advance of Christ's Church (Matthew 16:18). The world system that holds 11,000 people groups in darkness is "passing away."

We are winning.

As we fulfill our priestly duties of intercession for the nations, individuals in the presently unreached people groups will begin to respond to the Gospel proclaimed by cross-cultural missionaries. In fact, God makes it clear as he "registers the peoples" that even among people groups which ultimately reject Him, individuals will be saved. God says that "this one and that one" from even among the Babylonians and the Philistines were born in Zion—born again. These individuals will live side by side with believers of every people and tongue in Zion, the City of the New Jerusalem (Psalm 87:4–6).

As more and more individuals within a people group come to Christ, the satanic strongholds are weakened. An indigenous church is established; then more churches spring up in a church movement that can evangelize the entire people group. God's offer of the blessing of salvation in Christ can be heard in that people's own language in the context of its own culture. And whoever will call upon the name of the Lord will be saved.

But how can they call on a God they don't believe in?

And how can they believe in God if they don't hear about Him?

And how can they hear about Him without a proclaimer of the excellencies of this God who calls us out of darkness into His marvelous light?

And how can anyone proclaim this message to peoples among which Christ is not named—except they be sent?

Well?

For Further Thought

1. Take a full week to memorize Ephesians 6:10–19 and meditate on the necessity of being equipped for spiritual warfare.
2. Locate on a map the four countries with 85% of Latin America's unreached people groups—Guatemala, Ecuador, Bolivia and Peru.
3. Contact your mission agency working in one of these countries or contact the Adopt-A-People Clearinghouse, 1605 Elizabeth Street, Pasadena, CA 91104, U.S.A., to find the name of an unreached group in one of the four countries.

    Read through "How to Find Hidden Peoples in Your Library" (pp. 197, 198) and begin studying about the group you have selected. Keep a list of the key sources you find and forward that list to the agency you've linked up with.

As you study, pray specifically over each item you learn about that people. And pray the Lord of the Harvest to thrust out laborers to that group!

4. After a fairly thorough study of your people group, present your findings as interestingly as possible to a prayer group who will join you in the disciplines of spiritual battle over the future of that people.

CHAPTER 12

Action! What Now?
59 Action Steps for You
and Your Church

Y ou flew into Dallas last night, millions of lights twinkling across the Texas flatlands to welcome you home. But you've got one more appointment to keep across the grasslands into New Mexico. You want to meet the people involved in one of God's unusual chain of events as He unerringly accomplishes His purpose.

You've heard that a team of Native Americans helped establish one of the most significant churches in the world in the stark regions of central Asia, not far from where you began your global quest in Soviet Central Asia. You want to clarify the details of how the Navajo Indian Rodeo Ministry trek into Mongolia linked with a Washington D.C. man's testimony, in 1987, to a kid who, in 1980, in Moscow, had been given a Bible by a man from Tanzania, and then the tourists from Ohio—. You can't wait to meet Rick Leatherwood to get the details!

Today, the last day of your incredible journey around the globe, you're taking the train to Albuquerque. And as you slide along the sparse pastureland of gray-clouded West Texas, you feel worried about North America. It, together with Europe, is one of the Church's two slow-growth regions. The U.S. and Canada have been so blessed, and you now are clear on the Psalm 67 principle that God blesses us for a purpose—so that His way may be known on the earth, His salvation among all nations. You're also clear on the fact that to whom much is given, much is required. And you wonder how your own culture fits into God's big picture in the coming years.

Watching the cattle grazing along the rail line, you can't help but think of the history of the American character. Brash, obnoxious in so many foreign settings, stuck on the American way of doing things—

169

North Americans are often an irritating people to the other peoples of the earth. But they're also good-hearted. Tough, independent, ready to take on a challenge. Like the old frontiersmen, the settlers who moved West across the Great Plains to their manifest destiny, the entrepreneurs of the 1800's who invented everything from steamships to light bulbs, builders of the Panama Canal, the Rough Riders, the GIs of the great World Wars. North Americans are resourceful, greedy, kind, profane, God-fearing and addicted to pleasure all at the same time. What will God do with this hodge-podge people in His plans during the close of this millennium?

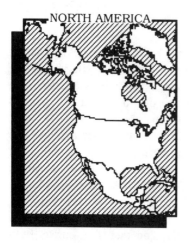

You're still mulling over such questions when you meet Rick Leatherwood, formerly with Navajo Gospel Mission and now with Mongolian Enterprises. In his early forties, Rick is a combination of Clint Eastwood and one of the Beach Boys—with a big blond mustache—one of those classic Americans with guts, brains and vision. Rick is a "wild man" with a yearning after God's heart for the nations.

"Yeah, I guess it was November tenth," he says as he throws your dented luggage into the back of his dented pickup. "Let me fill you in while we head out to the reservation. You can meet some of the team tonight."

November 10, 1990, was the date the first church was established among the Halh people. The Halh are the majority people group in Mongolia, which has always been cited as the world's most resistant and least evangelized country. As Rick tells it, the story borders on the bizarre.

A young Mongolian boy we'll call Yi, noted for his deft abilities in language-learning in the Soviet-controlled Mongolian Peoples' Republic, was sent to a Moscow university. There, in 1980, a native of Tanzania gave him an English Bible. "You can study English with it," the Tanzanian had said.

Yi studied English with the English Bible for seven years. He returned to Mongolia, and because of his fluent Russian and English, became one of the government's most-sought-after tour guides.

In 1987, U.S. tourist Doug Coe was in one of Yi's groups. Doug himself is a "wild man" of God. In the 70's when Watergate bad-guy Chuck Colson was born again and neither his old cronies nor the Christians would have anything to do with him, Doug Coe one day clomped into Colson's office, propped his cowboy boots up on the desk and drawled, "Well, welcome to the kingdom, brother!" Colson's outlook and ministry have never been the same. And Yi was never the same after sensing Coe's spirituality.

During a few seconds on the tour, Yi had a chance to ask Doug, "Do you know God?"

"Yes," Doug nodded.

Three hours later, Yi was able to whisper, "What is His name?"

"Jesus Christ," Doug said. And three days later, he had enough time with Yi to lead him to know Jesus Christ as Savior and Lord. "Don't worry," Doug told Yi. "I know it's illegal to be a Christian, and it will be hard for you. But friends will come."

Three years later, Yi was assigned another American tour group—this time an unusual Native American group representing Navajo, Winnebago, and several other Indian tribes. And it wasn't long before Yi realized that the Indians were believers; many of them from tribes that just decades ago were unreached themselves. In your research on unreached peoples, you know that in the U.S. more than 20 Native American reservations have no church! Twenty-nine more reservations each have at least one indigenous church, but in every case it's a church without the strength to evangelize its own people.

Yi found instant kinship, and he immediately arranged an audience with high-ranking government officials of Mongolia, to whom the group presented a just-translated Mongolian New Testament. Yi lined up a rodeo in which the celebrity Indians compared their trick-riding and rodeo skills with the best of the Mongols, descendants of the ancient horsemen of Genghis Khan, before a crowd of government officials and the press. The entire event was televised, including a ceremony in which the Americans sang the Lord's Prayer, interpreted on-camera by Yi, and signed the meaning of the song in Native American sign language.

After the rodeo, a local shepherd invited the Americans and most of the Mongolian press corps to dine with him. The shepherd slaughtered a goat for the feast. As the meal progressed in the shepherd's huge *ghur*, the Mongolians were astounded, as they passed slices of liver sandwiched between slabs of fat, to hear the Navajos say, "This is exactly how we eat!"

As he drives along, Rick Leatherwood is telling you that as he accompanied the American team, the affinity between the American Indians and Halh Mongolians was almost eerie. As you head north from Albuquerque, Rick finishes the story:

"At the end of the meal the shepherd, who had just lost a son the year before, brought into the *ghur* a tiny new lamb as a gift to my young daughter. I couldn't resist. I stood up, took the lamb in my arms and spoke through Yi to tell the crowd about God, whom they know as the creator-God—*Tinger*. God gave up His Son to die as the Lamb who could take away the sins of the world. I talked to them for about half an hour through Yi's interpretation. You could have heard a pin drop.

"And after such a well-illustrated sermon," Rick grins, "what could I do but give an invitation! I simply asked if anyone wanted to know more about receiving the forgiveness that the sacrifice of the Lamb of God brings. And before I could tell them what to do, every one of the 25 or so present raised his or her hand. We stood together—Mongol Halhs, American Navajos and Cocapaws, and Anglos. And we prayed."

Rick shakes his head. "In the week that followed, I spent hours and hours, day after day in the capital city of Ulan Bator with Yi. He was feverish to know everything I know about the Bible, how it all fits together. His thirst for spiritual knowledge was insatiable!

"Once in a while we'd take a break, go into the streets and pass out tracts and Scripture portions with other American teams—right in the capital of this country that a couple months ago would have jailed you if you tried to talk to anyone about Christ! The police even helped us figure out how best to do it without causing a riot!"

You finally ask, "And what about the church that was established?"

"Right," says Rick. "This bunch of Christians from Ohio, their luggage stuffed with tracts, pulls into the train station at Ulan Bator. Guess who just happens to be assigned as their tour guide? Right—our man Yi. Among the group are some pastors who meet with Yi and the other new Christians. They pretty thoroughly interview the new Mongolian believers and are amazed at Yi's years of Bible reading and bursts of spiritual insight. So, they all gather in a hotel room on November tenth, and climaxing a combination of events only the God of the Universe could concoct, they ordain Yi as elder of the first Mongolian church in the history of the world!"

———————

Tonight, after meeting with the Native American team just back again from Mongolia, you know you'll be ready to get home. You want to become active in this vast, global scheme as God plants just the right person in just the right place to reach whole people groups. You want to be just such a person, one whom God moves precisely into a specific niche in His great plan.

You can't wait to start seriously praying down the gates of hell, equipping the "sent-ones" in your fellowship, finding out what's happening in Uzbekistan since you left. And you know you won't have far to travel to start becoming active in blessing the world's remaining unreached peoples. Besides covering the globe in prayer, you know that dozens of unreached people groups are represented right here in North America in neighborhoods of almost every major metropolitan city, on the campuses of hundreds of universities, even on Native American Indian reservations!

———————

You're home. You're exhausted from your world travels. But you've caught a vision of God's heart for the nations. And you desperately want to do something about all you've been exposed to in your around-the-world quest to see what God is up to in His Word and in His works.

We'll list some possible action steps. But first let's think through some qualifiers.

Disclaimers for the To-Do List

1. *Remember the bigger picture of the big-picture-of-your-life purpose as you approach these action steps.*

The ultimate, eternal purpose for your existence is, according to the old confessions, to "glorify God and enjoy Him forever." God is shaping you toward your eternal character of being conformed to the image of Christ (Romans 8:29).

The big picture for your life here on earth is a subset of that ultimate purpose. God's global purpose of blessing you and using you to bless every people pulls billions into that ultimate purpose of glorifying God.

So, remember that accomplishing a list of very good things to tear down Satan's counter-kingdom and to offer the blessing of salvation to every people, though noble and vitally necessary, isn't as comprehensive as *being* a person who is growing in glorifying God and enjoying Him forever. Don't let your actions for global-purpose subvert the ultimate essence of God's work in you. *Selah* ("Pause and meditate on that one!").

2. Remember that an accurate, big-picture worldview integrates ministries; it doesn't eliminate them.

God fortunately didn't write the Bible in 100 topical sections. If He had, most of us would promptly turn to the topic that interests us most and we'd undoubtedly neglect the rest. We might excel in understanding the hypostatic union of Christ but never browse through the section on washing one another's feet.

God didn't organize the Word with a solid section of study on His heart for blessing the nations; instead He integrated that unchangeable purpose into passages dealing with His character, with obedience, and blindness, with the meaning of the Incarnation, with the growth of the Church, and so on. So the idea is this: Don't concentrate on your interest in, say, reaching the Bozos of Mali and conclude that the rest of the Church must then forget about discipling a younger brother, righting injustice, studying the Word, and feeding the homeless.

God's great purpose incorporates every God-given discipline in your life, every ministry in the life of your church. Think about it:

- God has gifted and interested several people in your fellowship to minister to the elderly shut-ins of your congregation. Rather than chastise such folk that they should instead be polishing pith helmets bound for Bhutan, think integration: God has blessed North American believers with a growing population of the very elderly. Why? Why hasn't He simply begun to take them home to heaven as He did during the first century when the average lifespan was 28? Clearly, God is blessing the elderly with time, with old age for His great, unchangeable purpose.

  When your church's shut-in visitation team visits to share songs and hold hands and listen to reminiscences, they can bring specific prayer requests of the urgent needs of the unreached peoples of the world. They can school the elderly in how to pray against the strongholds of Satan over a particular people group your church and mission is targeting. The team can infuse into each shut-in's remaining days the magic elixir of purpose—"You can spend time in prayer that we can't! You know more about the ups and downs of life than we do; you can pray specifically for the ups and downs of the mission team targeting this unreached group. You can help break open the way for the Gospel in this group as you pray against the principalities and powers that rule and blind them! We need you!" A church shut-in ministry can—and must—be incorporated into the vision of Christ's global cause.

- You and/or others in your fellowship may be zealous in the movement against pornography. Does this effort fit into the parameters of God's commands to "purge the evil among you" (Deuteronomy 13:5)? Of course it does. Does it fit into God's command to uplift the character of His name as His people take a stand for righteousness? Yes. Then, as His people serve the nations as a kingdom of priests, this Christian effort to abolish the abuse of women and children underscores God's people's stand for holiness.

  David sang, "He guides me in the paths of righteousness"—why? Not so I'll have an easy life; men love darkness rather than light, and the world system is programmed by its ruler to hate believers who stand for what's right. The paths of righteousness don't lead down Easy Street. "He guides me in the paths of righteousness for *His name's sake!*" (Psalm 23:3) Since Western pornography is one of the most offensive reasons the earth's one billion Muslims scorn "Christianity," the fight against pornography is essential in the proclaiming the excellencies of God's great name—His character—to reach every nation including the thousands of Muslim people groups.

- Your fellowship's women's group may enjoy baking, quilting, or other handcrafts. Great! Their personal worldviews may not yet center around God's unchangeable purpose, but their fundraising from the sale of such goodies and handcrafts can contribute greatly to the funding of a mission team targeting an unreached people.

  As a fellowship, make a list of all the various ministries going on in your church.

  Then think and pray through each ministry to determine just how it can be endued with the purpose of God's big picture. For example:

  Ministering toward healthy family lives and communicative

marriages is worthwhile not so much in order to give us easy, happy lives but rather to keep us from being derailed from serving in our part of His plan. Promoting physical fitness among believers has a big-picture purpose: To keep us from being distracted through health problems or weary from being out of shape as we pour our energies into our niche in His countdown to reach every nation. Learning how to counsel others about alternatives to abortion is grist for learning how to affect other people groups' birth-control problems and infanticide; what can we do about the abysmal abortion rate in China, for instance? Prayer sessions in the church should not be pleas for more blessings for ourselves; they should be the classic times in which we agree together to bind Satan's power over a people, to open blind eyes and deaf ears to the Gospel, to corporately strengthen those we are sending to the front lines.

Every God-ordained ministry of the church can be expanded as it aligns its purposes with the great, unchangeable purpose of God.

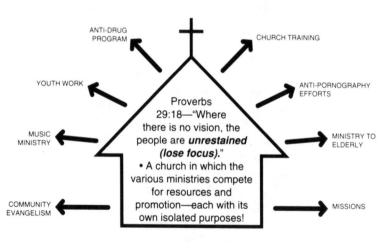

ministries from a church diagram

3. *Acknowledge the fact that to-do lists don't make you holy.*

Legalism is focusing on a few of God's laws and ignoring others. Legalism is formulating man-made rules and proclaiming them as "Thus saith the Lord." Legalism is appearing noble and spiritual in the

177

REACHING UNREACHED PEOPLES

EQUIPPING OTHER REACHED GROUPS TO
BECOME SENDING CHURCHES

BLESSING OUR OWN PEOPLE GROUP

Youth Work	Music Ministry
Missions	Community Evangelism
Ministry to Elderly	Anti-Pornography Efforts
Church Training	Anti-Drug Programs
Prayer Groups	12-Step Programs

A church in which the unchangeable *purpose* of God unites and integrates all the God-directed ministries, gifts and resources of the church.

"Record the vision… so the one who reads it may run" (Habakuk 2:2). A clear vision motivates the *whole* church!

whitewashed externals of your life and inside being filled with "dead men's bones." Personal holiness as a priest before your God won't come through following the suggestions of this or any other action list. Holiness and communion come through confession (1 John 1:9), through abiding in His Word (John 15:5–7), and through obedience of the heart (Isaiah 29:13).

So please do not consider this list of responses to a vision of God's global purpose as a kind of Protestant "penance." Following its every jot and tittle will get you nowhere in God's economy if your motives are unholy.

4. *Avoid Christian hedonism; avoid Christian asceticism.*

God will bless His people. We know this as the top-line of His unchangeable purpose. But to whine and beg that God will bless you with no thought of passing on His blessing to others is hedonism.

On the other hand, to refuse to accept God's blessing is the other extreme. Focusing solely on the bottom-line of blessing others can easily lead to a grandly humble Christian asceticism. Some Christians, including some missionaries, revel in their poverty, in their thoroughly inconvenient lives as if God's top-line blessing isn't to be enjoyed. God's pleasure-principle is a bit surprising; He wants us to accept His blessings—"In [His] right hand are pleasures forever" (Psalm 16:11). A simple lifestyle is commendable; but when it becomes a ritualistic "Don't touch; don't taste; don't handle," God says it's commendable only as a show of will-worshiping discipline and has nothing to do with real godliness! (See Colossians 2:20–23.)

So remember that moderation in all things—balance—is the key: Accept and enjoy God's blessings without guilt. Don't pretend that you're Ezekiel when it comes to guessing about other Christians' spirituality and heaping guilt on them whenever they enjoy God's blessing. (Very few of God's people since the day the scriptural canon was completed have been given responsibility to be God's one spokesperson to the entire people of God. Remember: No matter how devoted you are, you're no Habakkuk.) Proclaim the balance of God's top-line, bottom-line blessing, and balance your own life to pass on His blessings directly or indirectly to every people.

5. *Be strategic.*

Some ministries are good. Some are critical. As you pray through your response over the coming years to a vision of God's heart for the remaining unreached peoples of the earth, get strategic.

You are endowed with certain skills, heritage, interests, and spiritual gifts in a combination that no one in history has ever had. You are one of a kind; and what you do to fulfill your part in God's global plan is critical. So be yourself; adapt the ideas in the following action list to fit you and your abilities. Don't settle for a one-size-fits-all response to the vision. And don't be cornered by those who say, "Everyone should be a missionary"; "You should spend three hours a day praying for laborers or you are not dedicated"; "If you have a heart for the world, you should live like the poor, or at least give that appearance—never, *never* drive a new car."

Being strategic in your global ministry also means using discernment in where and how you focus your efforts. Many good and well-meaning ministries in North America describe their work as "missions," but have nothing to do with God's biblical mission to offer salvation to every last people group on earth. Others don't claim to be mission-oriented, and yet contribute in significant ways—perhaps indirectly—to reaching the unreached. Still other ministries claim to be focused on "unreached people," and yet by that they mean any individual who isn't a Christian. You can do a lot of good working with these ministries. Or you can do a lot of strategic work by evaluating your efforts according to two criteria:

1. *Does this effort indirectly or directly impact the final task of establishing a church movement among an unreached people group?*

Use your head here: Praying for a professor in a Bible school ministering within a reached people group such as the Spanish-speaking population of Honduras might seem non-strategic. But as that professor plants the vision in his Honduran students to go to North Africa and reach Muslim people groups—as hundreds of Hondurans have already done—your prayer efforts are absolutely strategic! Don't jump to conclusions when evaluating the critical impact of any ministry.

2. *Does this effort seek closure?*

The term is arbitrary; the hoped-for A.D. 2000 date of closure is arbitrary, but the meaning is important. Make sure you engage in a response to the vision in a way and with a group that intends to help get the job done. Sometimes legitimate ministries simply want to establish themselves as ongoing institutions. The lost will always be there; it's all sort of hopeless anyway, right? Wrong. Unfortunately these groups sometimes feel more urgency about their own fiscal condition than the fact that 55,000 people die daily without ever hearing the name of Christ. It's a good rule of thumb to judge whether you in your personal plans or the organizations you link up with mean business: Does this effort further the completion of the Great Commission?

So get strategic. Do as Cameron Townsend, founder of Wycliffe Bible Translators advised: "Find something no one else is doing. Then do it!"

Build and Act on the Vision: A To-Do List
Individual Action Steps

Commit Yourself
- Write a letter to a distant best friend telling of your commitment to the vision of God's great purpose on earth.
- List your top-line blessings and pray/meditate on how you can consecrate each one as a bottom-line blessing. Your life is a big "reception": What do you have that you have not received? How can these blessings be channeled into God's unchangeable purpose?

> spiritual gifts
> ethnic heritage
> big events that have shaped you (even negative events)
> education
> family traditions
> physical skills, talents
> supportive friends

- Explore your role as a "priest" (1 Peter 2:9, 10). What does a priest do? How can you literally or figuratively perform those services for the unreached peoples of the world? The consecration rites of the sons of Aaron lasted seven days. What could you do daily for a week that would cement in your memory the fact that you are one of a people of God's own possession, a holy nation, a kingdom of priests?
- List activities you can do away with to better commit your time to God's purpose.
- Sign what is known as the "Caleb Declaration" of commitment:

Then Caleb quieted the people before Moses, and said, "We should by all means go up and take possession of it, for we shall surely overcome it" (Numbers 13:30).

By the grace of God and for His glory, I commit my entire life to obeying His commission of Matthew 28:18–20, wherever and however He leads me, giving priority to the peoples currently beyond the reach of the Gospel (Romans 15:20, 21).

As an expression of my commitment, I will attempt to fulfill the following:

---

1. I will go to another culture or stay in my own, depending on the Lord's leading.
2. I will share my vision with other Christians, recognizing that my local church or campus student group are the obvious places for me to begin.
3. As others grow in commitment to Christ's global cause, I will trust that three of them will sign the Caleb Declaration.
4. To help me follow through with my commitment, I will "report" to someone—perhaps my pastor—monthly on how I am building and acting on this vision to reach every nation.

Signature _____

Date _____

(Consider photocopying this declaration and posting it where you'll see it often.)

- Raise a monument to your commitment (see Joshua 4): Actually build a monument (a pile of stones? a plaque? a slab of wet concrete?) to acknowledge your determination to align your life with God's unchangeable purpose; then annually spend a full day commemorating and renewing your commitment.
- If there is a possibility of your going to work cross-culturally here or abroad, ask around for a mission mentor you can be accountable to. Ask locally first, then check with your denomination. Finally, a national tracking and advising system operated by Caleb Project, P.O. Box 101239, Denver, CO 80250, U.S.A., will encourage you to progress in your commitment levels.

Share

- Compile your list of top-line blessings (see Commit Yourself) and ask others for clues to other blessings you're not realizing in your life. You'll then have to explain the "blessed to be a blessing" principle!
- Find one or two friends who will meet with you for a regular (weekly? bi-weekly? monthly?) unreached-peoples prayer session. As you develop as a small group:

  Help each other clarify your motives in mission-interest.
  Hold each other accountable for Bible study, prayer and giving.
  Encourage one another with global breakthroughs.

- Set up a monthly global-awareness book table in your church narthex. Set out pamphlets from your church's mission organizations, video and audio tapes, and study books to encourage others to catch the vision. Compile your own materials or contact William Carey Library, Box 40129, Pasadena, CA 91114, U.S.A. for information on a prepackaged library of materials called a World Christian Display Table.

Pray

- Set up a "Nation's Prayer Reminder" system—perhaps as simple as a card with one unreached people group listed—to prod your prayers while you are doing dishes, taking a shower, jogging, etc.
- Put a sticky label-dot on your watch, your clock at home or work and/or your car's rearview mirror to remind you to pray for the Lord of the harvest to thrust forth laborers.
- Communicate your commitment to pray for your church and denominational department or the mission agency you support.
- Subscribe to the *Global Prayer Digest*. This monthly prayer guide features an unreached people group each day. You can join with thousands of other prayer warriors focusing on that group that day. Send for a sample or subscribe for $6.00 per year from *Global Prayer Digest* Subscriptions, 1605 Elizabeth St., Pasadena, CA 91104, U.S.A., phone: 818/398-2249.
- Get the book *Operation World: A Day-to-Day Guide to Praying for the World* by Patrick Johnstone to further guide your prayers for the unreached peoples of the earth. Order from your local Christian book-

store or WEC International, Box 1707, Fort Washington, PA 19034, U.S.A.

- Beginning with those profiled in this book, pray over a list of unreached peoples. (See "How to Pray for Unreached Peoples," page 195). Once a month pray for them all at once, finding their locations on a world map. Perhaps "tithe" a Sunday and spend one-tenth of your day in prayer for the nations.
- Attend a "Concert of Prayer" with your family or a group of friends. These area-wide prayer gatherings concentrate on revival, leading to "fullness" (God's blessing on His people) and "fulfillment" (His blessing on every people). Contact the U.S. national office of Concerts of Prayer for locations near you: Concerts of Prayer, John Quam, Pentagon Towers, PO Box 36008, Minneapolis, MN 55435, U.S.A.

Study
- Review your understanding of the vision of "A Church for Every People by the Year 2000." Begin to memorize some of the focal passages cited in this study.
- Evaluate your personal study Bible—how many of the passages you have underlined refer to God's blessing the nations, and how many refer to God's blessing you?
- Buy a new Bible and underline the passages that specifically refer to God's blessing for the nations.
- Take the *Perspectives on the World Christian Movement* course that extensively covers the biblical, historical, cultural and strategic aspects of God's plan to reach every people, tribe, tongue and nation. Extension classes are offered throughout the world, and the course can be taken by correspondence. Contact the Perspectives Study Program, 1605 Elizabeth St., Pasadena, CA 91104, U.S.A., phone: 818/398-2125.
- Subscribe to a dozen or more mission magazines and newsletters. Some of the generic "must-reads" include:
    Mission Frontiers, Records Office, 1605 Elizabeth St., Pasadena CA 91104, U.S.A.
    Evangelical Missions Quarterly, Box 794, Wheaton, IL 60189, U.S.A.
    Pulse, Box 794, Wheaton, IL 60189, U.S.A.
- Read your Sunday newspaper and a national or large metropolitan Sunday newspaper to notice:

The hot spots of the news around the world—How could God be using this incident to further His unchangeable plan to bless the nations?

Any mention of unreached people groups—What is God doing among them? How is He using their problems and/or the wrath of men to accomplish His great purpose?

Determine how much time you'll devote weekly to think through world news relating to unreached people groups.

- Study what is happening in North American business abroad. Be aware of what North America is exporting; think through how that is affecting the nations and pray accordingly.

- Study the book *Serve As a Sender*, a surprising step-by-step approach to being a fully equipped sender to your missionaries. The book includes an eight-session study guide for groups. Order from Emmaus Road International, 7150 Tanner Court, San Diego, CA 92111, U.S.A., phone: 619/292–7020.

- Compile a cassette library of missiological tapes that focus on the biblical, historical, cultural and strategic factors of finishing the task of the Great Commission. As if you're on a self-study course and are cramming for a final exam, listen to these tapes while driving, jogging or doing house or yard work. Such tapes are available from William Carey Library, Box 40129, Pasadena, CA 91114, U.S.A. Ask for a resource catalog listing audio and video titles.

- Read and jot findings in books that focus on unreached peoples and finishing the task. An excellent basic library of these types of books is "The World Christian Bookshelf," with twelve basic books to study. Write or phone William Carey Library (818/798–0819) (address above) for further information.

- Go to school. For information on schools offering various mission training programs, send for a copy of the *Evangelical Missions Quarterly Guide to Continuing Education*, Box 794, Wheaton, IL 60189, U.S.A.

Align Your Lifestyle

- Evaluate the Christian records and books you own—how many of them are about God's top-line blessings? How many incorporate bottom-line topics? Work toward a balance in the input you and your family get from the music and literature in your home.

- Shop carefully for any item. Find the lowest price and give away what you saved!
- Collect your loose change daily, count it monthly and deposit it. Then send a check for that amount to an unreached peoples project championed by your mission agency.
- Find out the average salary of a minister in your denomination. If it is lower than your salary, adjust yours to his over a period of months or years. Perhaps by cutting $100 out of your budget each month or every two months you can reach the level of living of the average minister. Give what you save to your selected unreached peoples mission effort!
- Consult a financial planner and get help setting up a specific plan to decrease debt and increase your giving to the frontier mission efforts of your church or mission agency.
- Consider selling something you don't really need and giving the money to a team reaching an unreached people group you've been particularly burdened for.

Give Time
- Write to missionaries working on the front lines. Give personal news of the home front. Send the Sunday comics section of the newspaper or other section you know he/she may enjoy. Encourage. Don't expect an answer. Be cautious in writing any missionary working in restricted-access countries (check with your mission agency for guidelines).
- Connect with a mission agency wanting to learn more about a particular unreached group and clip newspaper and magazine references about that people and its geographical area. Don't forget that many, if not most, mission groups don't share much information; and breakthroughs reported in one denominational newsletter might be exactly the information another denominational mission department desperately needs! Be the information link for your agency!
- Volunteer five hours weekly to your church or mission agency in some effort to reach unreached peoples—regardless of how indirect it may be.
- Visit your nearest Christian radio station and encourage them to air mission programs on unreached people groups. Some "generic" mission programs that don't request funds include: "Around the World" with NewService 2000; "World Prayer 2000" with Jack McAlister.

The address for both is 1605 Elizabeth St., Pasadena, CA 91104, U.S.A. Also, brief glimpses of unreached peoples are heard on *Global Prayer Digest* Radio Spots sponsored by Far East Broadcasting Corporation's Mission Vision Network, Box 1, La Mirada, CA 90637, U.S.A.

- Volunteer to help in your local or regional international student ministry. Shock foreign students by showing interest in not only what political country they are from but what people group they are from. If you find students who are from people groups that have no strong Christian witness, relay this information to the international student organization headquarters, your mission agency and the Adopt-A-People Clearinghouse, 1539 E. Howard St., Pasadena, CA 90114, U.S.A.

  Offer these students a special gift of an English dictionary. But give a very special one—the *All Nations English Dictionary*, a dictionary prepared by All Nations Literacy. In addition to the thousands of regular entries, every term that relates to salvation in Christ provides a definition and a surprisingly full explanation of that topic from the biblical perspective. Words such as Christ, save, glory, heaven, grace, sin, commandment, and so on, give a diligent user the complete Gospel! This brilliant, 756-page dictionary is available singly or by group discount from All Nations, Box 41540, Pasadena, CA 91114, U.S.A.

  Remember, you just may be hosting an international student who could be the first one of his/her people to come to Christ. Mission groups targeting that people group will be more than interested in following up on that individual—learning language nuances, customs, and other valuable "inside" information. Perhaps that one student will be the key, the evangelist who will plant a church and foster a movement to Christ in his own people group!

- Find out if there are internationals from unreached people groups working or living in your community. Remember that individuals from most Muslim, Hindu and Buddhist peoples will be from unreached groups. Develop relationships with these internationals, realizing again that they may be precisely the one family God has ordained to carry the Gospel back to their homeland! Give a gift of the *All Nations English Dictionary* as noted above. Then contact Doorstep Opportunities for ideas on how to best minister cross-culturally in your area. Write Doorstep Opportunities, 1605 Elizabeth St., Pasadena, CA 91104, U.S.A.

- Use your vacation time to help research an unreached people group or assist in pre-evangelism (relief work, literature distribution, etc.) in a major city with unreached people communities, or overseas. Contact your unreached peoples-focused mission agency for opportunities. Get a clear idea of short-terming opportunities in *Stepping Out: A Guide to Short-Term Missions* available through William Carey Library (address given previously).

- Help with research. Link up with your mission agency or a group such as the Adopt-A-People Clearinghouse (address given previously) and discover what needs to be found out about a particular people group. You'll be amazed at how much strategic research needed by the mission community has already been done in decades' worth of sociological and anthropological studies just sitting in your nearest university library! (See "How to Find Hidden Peoples in Your Library," page 197, for specific research ideas.)

- Draw a timeline of your life from birth to death. Consider tithing a tenth of your "expected" lifetime to be involved full-time in sending or going. (With all we've studied, are you still waiting for a "call" from heaven?)

- Contact a mission agency targeting unreached peoples and start corresponding about possible short-term or career assignments.

- Research the possibilities of becoming a part-time or full-time mission mobilizer in your area. Learn how to share the vision with groups. Encourage prayer, giving and activism on behalf of the unreached. Contact your mission agency for ideas. Or, to become a "generic" mission mobilizer representing all evangelical mission groups, write Regional Office Coordinator of the U.S. Center for World Mission for information on serving in your area. Also, the Mobilization Division of the U.S. Center for World Mission can equip you with materials to encourage churches to "adopt" an unreached people group. Write and ask for an Adopt-A-People Advocate Kit. The U.S. Center address is 1605 Elizabeth St., Pasadena, CA 91104, U.S.A.

Action Steps for Your Fellowship Group or Church

Build a big-picture foundation of education.

Work with others, particularly the leadership of your church or fellowship group, to initiate the following educational steps in your group. Each of these resources is available through the U.S. Center for

World Mission or a cooperating organization. For information on resources, contact the Mobilization Division, U.S. Center for World Mission (address given previously), phone: 818/398–2200. Ask how your association or denomination can customize and/or translate these resources for your own groups and churches.

1. Post *Unreached Peoples Posters* around your facility. These striking posters map out the details of the remaining task of reaching every people group for Christ. Also display a huge, informative *Bibles for All Map* of the world and its unreached.

2. Set out *Catch the Vision* brochures. These comprehensive pamphlets overview the biblical and strategic vision of finishing the task of the Great Commission. (Available in 10-packs.)

3. Host a "Sunday for the World." This is a one-Sunday mission emphasis on the challenge of planting a church among each of the remaining unreached people groups. The packet includes Sunday school lessons for all ages, sermon outlines and samples, bulletin inserts for note-taking and responses, a small-group Bible study guide on unreached peoples and take-home prayer guides for the family. A stunning one-day mission emphasis!

4. Use the *Catch the Vision 2000* study course in adult Sunday school, home-group Bible studies, midweek services, or Sunday evening sessions. The complete 12-session curriculum manual can be used with or without each participant having a *Catch the Vision 2000* text.

   Or, for an even more intensive study of God's unchangeable purpose to bless every people with His offer of salvation, study through the video-based course *Destination 2000*—a 12-session group study based on the book *Destination 2000*.

5. Initiate a monthly mission fellowship in your church to study the implications of the biblical, historical, cultural and strategic aspects of God's global purpose. The mission fellowship curriculum *Vision for the Nations* is a perfect program that provides video-based teaching, guides for group discussion, instructions on how to pray daily for unreached peoples and a plan for actually "adopting" an unreached people group. These twelve 90-minute sessions form an entire year's worth of big-picture education!

   Also available are *WorldView Videos*—rough-cut footage fresh from the field of unreached people groups. These are stunning visualizations of unreached peoples—perfect for monthly mission fellowships, family prayer times, classroom use, reference in your church flibrary, study discussion starters.

6. Since as a group you're getting out of the pew and into the battle-field, study through the nine-session video course *Spiritual Warfare*.

7. As a group, study the clear, strategic how-to's of equipping and wholly supporting your mission teams on the field with the 8-session book and course *Serving As Senders*.

8. Begin to work and pray through the nuts-and-bolts manual *How to Adopt a People*.

9. Offer or collaborate with other churches to offer a *Perspectives on the World Christian Movement* course in your area.

Next, begin to amplify and expand on your mission educational foundation by hosting incisive seminars on various aspects of reaching the unreached. Some basic seminars—ideal for inviting others to catch the foundational vision of God's global plan—include:

- *Catch the Vision 2000* Seminar
- *Destination 2000* Seminar
- *The 4,000-Year Connection* Seminar
- A Mini-Perspectives Seminar
- *For Those Who Go*: Getting beyond Romanticism in missions.
- *Serving As Senders*: How to support your missionaries while they prepare to go, while they are on the field and when they return home.

Other more specific aspects of what God is doing today are presented in high-level seminars including:

- Muslim Awareness Seminars
- China Awareness Seminars
- An Introduction to Cross-Cultural Ministry Seminars
- "Nothing Good Just Happens:" How to Mobilize Your Church for Missions—a seminar workship for church leaders

For information on booking any of the above seminars, contact the U.S. Center for World Mission, Mobilization Division, who will put you in touch with the organizations offering each.

10. As a church, study your church's mission efforts:
- How can you better pray for and equip your missionaries to reached peoples, in order that they might encourage nationals to

190

become sending churches—sending their own missionaries to unreached peoples?

- How can you better pray for and equip your missionaries working among unreached groups?

11. Initiate the strategies and planning in special handbooks from the Association of Church Missions Committees, Box ACMC, Wheaton, IL 60189–8000, U.S.A. Some of these include Your Church Missions Policy Handbook, Cultivating a Missions-Active Church, and Missions Conference Planner. For ongoing help in mobilizing your church, consider joining ACMC or the Association of International Mission Services organization for charismatically oriented congregations, AIMS, Box 60534, Virginia Beach, VA 23464, U.S.A.

12. Help organize a "Concert of Prayer" in your area to focus every evangelical church in the region on the crucial role of corporate prayer in blessing the nations. Perhaps your city will soon be hosting Concerts of Prayer as is done in Minneapolis, where more than 10,000 regularly gather to pray in concert for the completion of the final task! (address given in individual action list.)

13. Take accountability to link with a mission agency targeting a specific people group; "adopt" a people! The varying degrees of responsibility your church can assume in this demanding enterprise are determined by you as a church and the agency. Contact your unreached-people-targeting mission agency or the Adopt-A-People Clearinghouse.

14. Send your pastor(s) to visit the field. Nothing will infuse church leadership with a vision to complete the Great Commission as convincingly as firsthand experience in researching or visiting an unreached group.

15. Send your pastor or other church leader for a month or two to a mission agency—perhaps even to do clerical work! Nothing will enable your church leadership to sympathize more with the demands of mission work than seeing the support system operations at agency headquarters.

16. Send your pastor to the *Perspectives on the World Christian Movement* intensive course held each January on the campus of the U.S. Center for World Mission in Pasadena, California. Contact the Perspectives Study Course offices at the U.S. Center address for details, or for the location of the Perspectives extension course offered nearest you.

*E*nough ideas to prod your thinking? Your own response to the vision of God's orchestration of world events to proclaim His character to every people, tribe, tongue and nation might never appear on such an action-step list. But since to whom much is given, much is required, your sense of that vision demands your response. What will you do?

If nothing else, do the foundational action step. Since you've had a chance to "look to the fields," do what Jesus commanded: "Beseech the Lord of the harvest to send out workers into His harvest" (Matthew 9:38). Pray!

As Mary simply put it: "Whatever He says to you, do it" (John 2:5). And let us know how it goes!

> Yours for the nations,
> Bill & Amy Stearns
> PO Box 416
> Colorado Springs, CO 80901-0416

For Further Thought

1. Look up each of the scripture references in this chapter to study context and specific meanings.
2. Get together with others in your church fellowship to list, as suggested, all the ministries going on in your church and how each can be imbued with the direction of God's unchangeable purpose.
3. Pray over the ideas you come up with. Pray over the individual and corporate action steps suggested and taken.
4. If you are not presently working through this book as part of a group study, contact your student group headquarters, denomination, association or mission agency for the *Catch the Vision 2000* 12-week curriculum. Or, order manuals for your group and others from the William Carey Library, P.O. Box 40129, Pasadena, CA 91114, U.S.A. (800/777–6371 or 818/798–0819).

CHAPTER 13

Resources for Building & Sharing the Vision!

These resources are available from your local Christian bookstore, through William Carey Library, a mission resource clearinghouse (P.O. Box 40129, Pasadena, CA 91114 USA, phone: 818/798–0819), or by calling 1–800–MISSION within the United States.

Books

Eternity in Their Hearts, Don Richardson (Regal Books)
From Jerusalem to Irian Jaya: A Biographical History of Christian Missions, Ruth Tucker (Zondervan)
Shadow of the Almighty: The Life and Testament of Jim Elliot, Elisabeth Elliot (Harper & Row)
Touch the World Through Prayer, Wesley Duewel (Zondervan)
Destined for the Throne, Paul Billheimer (Bethany House Publishers, Christian Literature Crusade)
Destination 2000, Bob Sjogren (Frontiers)
Serving as Senders, Neal Pirolo (Emmaus Road International)

Bible Studies

Journey to the Nations: A Study Guide for World Christians (Caleb Project)
Catch the Vision 2000!: A 12-session Study Guide (William Carey Library)
Destination 2000, a video-based 12-session study (Frontiers).

Daily Prayer Guides

Global Prayer Digest (William Carey Library)
Operation World: A Handbook for World Intercession, Patrick J. Johnstone (STL)

Maps, Posters

National Geographic "Peoples" Maps, (National Geographic Society)
"Bibles for All" wall map of the world's unreached and explanatory video (World Population Study Center)
"The Unreached Peoples Poster" with statistics of the task (William Carey Library)

Brochures, Articles

Catch the Vision! (William Carey Library)
O God, Revive Us Again, Rev. Will Bruce (Overseas Missionary Fellowship)
The Non-Essentials of Life, Roberta Winter (William Carey Library)
Four Men, Three Eras, Ralph Winter (William Carey Library)

Videos, Films

The Abraham Factor, Don Richardson (William Carey Library)
Jesus: Messiah for All Peoples, Don Richardson (William Carey Library)
Friends, InterVarsity Christian Fellowship (2100 Productions)
The Keith Green Memorial Concert (Last Days Ministries)
The Wait of the World (Gospel Films)
Peace Child (Gospel Films, Muskeegan, MI)
Gods of the New Age (Malaga Cove Pictures, Huntington Beach, CA)

Traveling Teams and Seminars

Contact your denomination or mission agency you support for speakers.

Caleb Project Traveling Teams—young adults accepted as mission agency candidates travel the country speaking to college fellowships, churches and other groups presenting the challenge of missions. Contact Caleb Project, P.O. Box 101239, Denver, CO 80250.

Destination 2000—a fast-paced, two-day seminar packed with the Bible and stories on God's unchangeable purpose to bless every people with His offer of salvation. Contact Bob Sjogren, Frontiers, 1610 Elizabeth St., Pasadena, CA 91104, phone: 818/398–2340.

The 4000-Year Connection—Don Richardson's gripping seminar of God's purpose and plan throughout history. Contact Don Richardson Ministries, Woodland Hills, CA 91364, phone: 818/346–3211.

Catch the Vision 2000! Seminar—the focus of this book is presented in a one-day seminar format for churches, fellowships, Bible studies, etc. Contact Bill and Amy Stearns, PO Box 416, Colorado Springs, CO 80901-0416.

Like It's 1999—a youth-oriented day of focus on finding your part in God's global plan! Contact Bill and Amy Stearns, (address given previously).

VISION
2000

How to Pray for Unreached Peoples

Prepare yourself as you, your church or fellowship prays for an unreached people. They will be difficult to pray for! Because they are unreached, we know very little about these groups. And the lack of personal, up-to-date information sometimes causes us to falter in disciplined intercession because our petitions are so vague, general, sometimes repetitious. Be forewarned: The less we know about the object of our prayers, the easier it is to forget altogether to pray, or to just give up.

But the very lack of information about an unreached people makes it more imperative that we do pray daily, or even several times a day, for that people. If we're really going to pray for a relatively unknown group, the only sure way is to do so daily, or even several times a day, until it is engrained into our consciousness.

What Do We Pray For? Perhaps you haven't been able to find much information on your adopted people's language, culture, habitat, mode of living, material and physical needs, etc. But you can find all sorts of in-depth information on them—in the Word. Basic, essential needs for prayer are listed clearly throughout Scripture; everything God says regarding the *ethne*—the "nations," the "peoples," the "gentiles"—reveals His will for them. "And this is the confidence which we have before Him, that, if we ask anything according to His will, He hears us. And if we know that He hears us in whatever we ask, we know that we have the requests which we have asked from Him" (1 John 5:14,

15). Always have your Bible handy when praying for your adopted people; it will help you to pray more intelligently for God's will to be accomplished among them.

1. Pray for workers—for Christians from other people groups who are living in the same country, missionaries from other countries in the Third World, and North American missionaries. (See Matthew 9:37, 38.)

2. Pray for any existing churches in that country to get a missionary vision for reaching that particular unreached people.

3. Pray for a "door of utterance." (See Colossians 4:3, 4.) This is a two-sided door: The door of the speaker and the door of the hearer. The message must be understandable to the hearer. It must be an answer to his felt need—not what the speaker thinks is his felt need. You know that these people probably do not readily welcome foreigners or warm up to ideas of changing their "religion." You can pray that God will prepare hearts to receive His messengers, His message, and His Son as their Savior.

4. You know that your adopted people group, like all peoples without Christ, are walking according to the course of this world—carried about by what everyone else is doing.

   You can pray that when God's messengers arrive, there will be those who will dare to go against the grain of peer pressure and receive God's servants graciously and listen to their message.

5. You know that the "prince of the power of the air" has complete dominion over them.

   So you must intercede, entering into the spiritual warfare that surrounds the messengers and the recipients of the Gospel. You can pray that God will "bind the strong man of the house" so his possessions can be taken from him. And when you enter into spiritual warfare for unreached peoples, remember to pray for your own protection, as you too may be under attack from the enemy.

6. Pray that new believers will make a complete break with ancestral practices, which will release them from the power of the spirits over them. Pray that they will have the assurance: "Greater is He that is in you than he that is in the world."

7. Pray that an evangelizing, reproducing church will be planted among them, and that new converts will grow in the grace and knowledge of Christ.

8. You know that God has promised all the nations, even the uttermost parts of the earth to His Son for an inheritance, a possession. (See Psalm 2.) You can pray that Christ will soon possess the inheritance that is rightfully His—including your adopted people group.

9. You know that it is God's eternal purpose to bring individuals from every *ethne* to Christ. You can pray that your adopted people will soon be represented along with all the other nations in the Body of Christ. (See Revelation 5:9; 7:9.)

10. Keep praying for the nations according to the will of God, as revealed in Scripture, for the very individuals now moving through their time on earth plagued with the fear, pain and uncertainty of a life and an eternity without Christ.

How to Find Hidden Peoples in Your Library

Allan Starling directs the Field Division of Gospel Recordings. He is the editor of *Seeds of Promise* and the *Peoplesfile* Index. The following is an article adapted from *Peoplesfile Index*, 1986 Edition, published by Global Mapping International and is used by permission.

"The whole earth was of one language and of one speech. . . . And the Lord said, 'Come, let us go down and there confuse their language so that they cannot understand one another's speech.' So the Lord scattered them . . . upon the face of all the earth" (Genesis 11:1, 7, 8, New KJV).

When God does a job, He does it well! Today, thousands of years after Babel, the world is still scattered with such a confusion of peoples and languages that even the experts find it hard to agree on just how many there are and how they are related. The very names of these groups are "confused"; one group may be known by as many as five different names. Yet God's love extends to each people, and He is "not willing that any should perish."

As followers of Christ, we have our orders to reach all these peoples with the good news of the Gospel. In recent years Christians around the world have become increasingly aware of the need to identify these groups and to ask a number of questions: "Who are they? Where are they? How many of them are there? What do they believe? Is anyone reaching out to them with the Gospel?"

We have also come to acknowledge our need for a definition of "people group." Attempts at definition will differ greatly, depending

198

on whether you consult an anthropologist, linguist, sociologist, missionary, or government census official! The following two definitions (cited in, among other sources, *Unreached Peoples '83*) have been widely accepted in evangelical mission circles and are phrased from the viewpoint of evangelism:

People Group: A significantly large sociological grouping of individuals who perceive themselves to have a common affinity for one another. From the viewpoint of evangelization this is the largest possible group within which the Gospel can spread without encountering barriers of understanding or acceptance.

Unreached People Group: A people group among which there is no indigenous community of believing Christians with adequate numbers and resources to evangelize this people group without outside (cross-cultural) assistance.

Defining and identifying peoples is only the first step in a process, but it is nevertheless an important step and something that has never been totally accomplished. Fortunately, several mission-related research organizations are currently focusing on this task. The job is far from done, and these organizations deserve our strong support.

In the meantime, where does that leave you? Let's assume that you have heard about a group called the Danakil, reported to live somewhere in Eastern Africa. You feel that God wants you to be involved in reaching them with the Gospel. How can you find out more about them? Where do you start?

Fortunately, much of the information is out there, waiting for someone like you to find it. Think of it as a treasure hunt. All you need is a set of clues, some time, and a heap of patience and persistence. I'd be most delighted to accompany you, so let's do it together.

PART I: ESTABLISHING THE CLUES

Before we start on our treasure hunt, we need some clues. These clues about the Danakil can be obtained through the *Peoplesfile Index* and the three major publications (described below) it references. These publications may not be available at your local library, but you can check with mission offices and Bible school libraries. You can also order them at the addresses given below:

1. *Ethnologue* (1984): lists 5,445 language groups, showing the number of speakers, locations, dialects, and Bible translation status.

Also available is a separate index listing all languages and dialects. Order from the Summer Institute of Linguistics, 7500 West Camp Wisdom Rd., Dallas, TX 75236, U.S.A.

2. *Recorded Language Directory*: lists over 4,300 languages and dialects recorded by Gospel Recordings, together with alternate names. Order from Gospel Recordings, 122 Glendale Blvd., Los Angeles, CA 90026, U.S.A.

3. *Unreached Peoples Annual* (1985): Annuals in this series have been published since 1979. In addition to general articles, they contain lists of over 3,800 groups reported as unreached. Order from MARC, 919 W. Huntington Dr., Monrovia, CA 91016, U.S.A.

4. *The Peoplesfile Index*. The main objective of this publication, published in September 1986, is to help you find more information on unreached peoples. In addition, you'll find the following:

- A list of all peoples and languages in a given country;
- A global index of all possible names for languages, dialects and peoples;
- A cross-reference to show how they are listed in other publications;
- An indication of the status of each group, showing those that are reported to be unreached, have the Gospel on audio recordings, have a Bible or portion of Scripture in their own language, are reported to have translation needs, or that have a need for both a Bible translation and recording.

Order from Global Mapping International, 1605 Elizabeth St., Pasadena, CA 91104.

Checking *Peoplesfile*, we discover these clues about the Danakil:

Clue # 1: All three source publications use Afar as the primary name.

Clue # 2: The Afar (Danakil) are reported to be unreached.

Clue # 3: Gospel Recordings has made recordings of the Afar language.

Clue # 4: Bible portions are available in Afar.

Clue # 5: The group can be found in Djibouti, Ethiopia, and Somalia.

Clue # 6: The group is known as Afar, Adal, Afaraf, Afarafa, and Danakil.

Checking the *Ethnologue*, we make some additional discoveries:

Clue # 7: The Afar are a nomadic people.

Clue # 8: Saho is a related but distinct group.

Clue # 9: The following agencies are working among the Afar: SIM, CMML, OPC, RSM, ECMY. (We'll find out the meaning of these acronyms later.)

Checking the *Unreached Peoples Annuals* (see clue #2), we further find:

Clue #10: *Unreached Peoples '79* has an expanded description of the Afar.

Clue #11: The Afar are a Muslim group.

Let's use some of these clues to find more information about the Afar. As I've mentioned, the three publications referenced by the *Peoplesfile Index* will not be found in most public libraries. However, other sources can be found in public and private libraries, obtained through inter-library loan or purchased. Now we are finally ready for the library.

PART II: SEARCHING THE LIBRARY

We need to remind ourselves of some basics. First, don't expect to find all the resources mentioned here in every library. If possible, find a university library or main city library, or perhaps the library of a mission office. Even if you can only find a few of the resources mentioned, you might still be able to build a good picture of the people you are researching. Also remember, that unless you have a library card, you won't be able to borrow books, but since many libraries have photocopy machines, take plenty of change for making copies.

We need to give ourselves plenty of time at the library—a whole day if possible. "Finding" unreached peoples isn't always easy. It's going to take some patient research, and we're going to have to look in several places.

Let's break up our search into a number of steps:

Step 1: Determine the search procedure. We'll use this procedure in each of the following steps. Unless we are looking for a large group, it's likely that we won't immediately find what we want because the information will be hidden in some volume or periodical. (Is that why they call them "hidden" peoples?) We start with the specific and move to broader categories as necessary. Here are the categories we choose in our search for the Afar: (a) Afar, Danakil (clue #1); (b) Nomads (clue #7); (c) Saho (clue #8); (d) Muslim or Islam (clue #11); (e) Ethnology; (f) Anthropology; (g) Djibouti, Ethiopia, Somalia (clue #5); (h) Other names for Afar, e.g., Danakil (clue #6).

Step 2: Check the *National Geographic Magazine Index*, published by the National Geographic Society, Washington, D.C. 20036, U.S.A. This index of articles from 1947 tells us of an article called "The Danakil: Nomads of Ethiopia's Wasteland," to be found in the February 1970 issue. We'll look forward to enjoying this magazine's usual high-quality color photographs as well as the text.

Step 3: Check the *Encyclopedia Britannica*, Index Volume. The Encyclopedia has a surprising amount of information about peoples and countries. In the Index volume, under "Afar," we see a listing for an article entitled "Saho-Afar." There is also more information under "Ethiopia: the People." In addition, we are told that the Afar are Sunni Muslims and that we can get more information under "Islam."

Step 4: Check *Muslim Peoples*, Richard V. Weekes, Editor. The second edition of this world ethnographic survey has been revised and expanded to two volumes. It contains maps showing the general location of Muslim groups, and documents 190 ethnic and/or linguistic groups that are totally or partially Muslim. Volume 1, page 10, includes an article on the Afar and a bibliography for further reading. An appendix listing Muslim ethnic groups by country tells us that the Afar constitute one of nineteen Muslim groups in Ethiopia.

Step 5: Check *Peoples of the Earth*, a set of 20 volumes published by Danbury Press. Each volume contains many general articles, thumbnail sketches, and photographs of people groups. This series is now out-of-print, but fortunately our particular library has a set. Continuing our quest for information on the Afar, we find (in Volume 2, page 22) an article on the Danakil and Saho (clue #8), complete with maps and pictures.

Step 6: Check the 20-volume *Illustrated Encyclopedia of Mankind*, published by Marshall Cavendish Ltd., 58 Old Compton St., London, W1V 5PA, United Kingdom. More than 500 peoples and cultures are represented. Yes, the Afar are there, too—on page 12 of Volume One.

Step 7: Check the *Library of Congress Subject Headings*. These are large-bound volumes, kept in most libraries, showing the subject headings used in the card catalog system. Even if our library doesn't use the Library of Congress system, this step is still useful. The headings in bold type are those used in the card catalog. Other names in the volume are related topics.

Under "Afar," we actually find a heading for "Afar Language (PJ2421)." Because our library uses Library of Congress codes, we can now go straight to the "PJ" section in the shelves and look for related books. If the library used the Dewey Decimal system, we would simply jot down the headings to use in the next step.

Sorry, there are no books we can use under the "PJ" section in our library, so let's look under a broader topic. There are a number of headings under "Muslim," and under "Ethiopia" we find "Ethiopian Languages (PJ8991–9)." Even though we are unsuccessful once again, we keep a note of these headings to use in the next few steps.

Step 8: Check the card catalog file. Let's remember to follow the procedure we set up in step one, aided by the subject headings we found in the last step. Whether the catalog file uses Dewey Decimal or Library of Congress codes, the procedure is the same. As soon as we find one volume in the card catalog that looks promising, we look for it as well as for other related volumes near it on that section of the shelves.

Step 9: Check the *Subject Guide to Books-in-Print*. The librarian shows us where to find these large-bound volumes. Once again, using our set procedure and our list of subject headings, we find the names of several books-in-print related to the Afar.

Step 10: Check the *Linguistic Bibliography*, edited by J. Beylsmit. This contains a listing of "all" the descriptions of known languages. Although the articles and books referred to may be technical in nature, many times they will include a section on the speakers of the language and give additional useful information.

Step 11: Check the *MARC* (MAchine Readable Catalog) fiche. If you're not familiar with fiche, it is a form of microfilm, but on 3 × 5 "cards." Our library has a microfiche reader handy. (By the way, don't confuse this MARC with the other MARC—Missions Advanced Research &

Communication Center—mentioned elsewhere!)

We check the Author/title first, once again using our set procedure. We come up with "Afar Depression in Ethiopia, #838 e 29." Next we check microfiche number 838, square e 29, and see a description of a book, that is not at all what we want. If it had been, we could have written down the Library of Congress and Dewey classifications that are given below the description. Oh well, we can't win them all!

Step 12: Check the periodicals guides. With our librarian's help, we find a number of periodical indexes in our library, notably, for our purposes, *Reader's Guide to Periodical Literature*, *Christian Periodical Index*, and *Social Sciences Index*.

Step 13: Check *Background Notes*, produced by the Bureau of Public Affairs of the United States Department of State. These are obtainable from the Superintendent of Documents, U.S. Government Printing Office, Washington, DC 20402. The notes give an overview of the geography, government, policies, economy, history and people of the country of your interest.

Step 14: Check the *Human Relations Area Files* (HRAF). This is only possible if you live in the U.S.A. and have access to certain major university libraries. The files contain detailed information on approximately 400 different cultures.

Step 15: Talk to the reference librarian. Before leaving the library, we talk to the librarian and explain what we are looking for and what we have already found. The more we know, the more the librarian can help us.

PART III: LOOKING FURTHER

We are finished in the library, but our research is not yet done. Other people, organizations, and publications can help us.

Step 16: Check mission agencies working in or near our people group. Remembering that missionaries are busy people, we do our homework first, then we send them a copy of our findings along with specific questions. If we can demonstrate that we are serious, they are more likely to spend time digging out additional information or checking what we have.

First we check the *Ethnologue* (page 577) for the full names of the missions working with our group (clue #9). Here they are:

CMML = Christian Missions in Many Lands (Plymouth Brethren)

ECMY = Evangelical Lutheran Church in Ethiopia

OPC = Orthodox Presbyterian Church

RSM = Red Sea Mission

SIM = SIM International (formerly Sudan Interior Mission)

We are surprised to find five groups working among the Afar. (This may not be very common among unreached peoples, but remember that the definition of an unreached people is based on the strength of the indigenous community of believing Christians in that group rather than on the amount of work being done in that group.) To get the mission addresses and find other possible agencies, we then check either or both of the following: (1) *Missions Handbook*, published by the Missions Advanced Research and Communication Center (MARC), 919 W. Huntington Drive, Monrovia, CA 91016, U.S.A; (2) *UK Christian Handbook*, published by Evangelical Alliance, 186 Kennington Park Rd., London SE11 4BT, United Kingdom. Both handbooks contain listings of people groups by organization as well as by country.

Step 17: Learn more about the areas where our group is located. Some of these references may be in your library. You may have to order or borrow others:

(a) *Operation World*, by Patrick Johnstone, STL Publications, PO Box 48, Bromley Kent, England. Here is a popular and highly readable survey of the basic prayer needs of each country of the world, supplemented by information on population, ethnic groups, economy, religions and political situations.

(b) *World Christian Encyclopedia*, edited by David B. Barrett, Oxford University Press. "The heart of the Encyclopedia is a detailed, country-by-country survey of Christianity and other religions . . . including political, demographic, linguistic, ethnic and cultural data . . ." and much, much more.

Checking under "Djibouti" and "Ethiopia," we find, for instance, that the Danakil comprise 35.1% of the population of Djibouti and 0.9% of the population of Ethiopia. Finding "Afar" in the index on page 988, we see a code of CMT33z that leads us to page 113. There we read that the Afar are categorized as "other Cushitic," and are also called the Danakil. The table on page 787 tells us that the Afar are part of a larger grouping of 25 people groups speaking 20 languages. We note that this major grouping is only 1.41% Christian, and, since the word "Christian" here represents a very broad category, we conclude that there are extremely few evangelicals among them.

(c) *World Christianity Series*, published by MARC (address given previously). This series of four large paperbacks gives a survey of the status of the Christian faith in various world regions. Currently available: Central America and the Caribbean; Eastern Asia; Middle East; and South Asia.

(d) Other references include area handbooks, *Encyclopedia of the Third World*, and *Encyclopedia Britannica* (or other encyclopedias).

Step 18: Check with agencies doing research on unreached peoples. In most cases this can be a two-way street. Not only can you ask for specific information, but you can also help to update or correct existing data. The first four groups have questionnaires for use in gathering data:

(a) The Adopt-A-People Clearinghouse, 1605 Elizabeth St., Pasadena, CA 91104, U.S.A. Ask if any churches have "adopted" the people group you're researching.

(b) *Ethnologue*, 7500 W. Camp Wisdom Rd., Dallas, TX 75236, U.S.A. This volume is available for $18.00 (U.S.). Address questions to the editor and direct orders to the bookstore, both at the same address.

(c) Gospel Recordings, Field Division, 122 Glendale Blvd., Los Angeles, CA 90026, U.S.A. Request the latest recorded language directory for a particular country, a catalog of available audio tools, or obtain information on a specific recorded language.

(d) Research institutes located at the U.S. Center for World Mission, 1605 Elizabeth St., Pasadena, CA 91104 U.S.A. These separate but collaborating agencies include the Sonrise Center for Buddhist Studies, Institute of Chinese Studies, Institute of Hindu Studies, Institute of Latin American Studies, Institute of Tribal Studies, and the Samuel Zwemer Institute for Muslim Studies. Check for specific information on peoples, ask about seminars and courses offered, and request descriptions of available materials.

(e) WEC International Research Office, Bulstrode, Gerrards Cross,

Bucks SL9 8SZ, United Kingdom. This office is directed by Patrick Johnstone, author of *Operation World*.

WHAT NOW?

Now that we have the information, what are we going to do with it? That is a question that only you, with the Lord's guidance, can answer. There are, however, several things I would reiterate:

- Help The Adopt-A-People Clearinghouse to update their files. Send them corrections or additions on the forms they'll provide.
- Pray for unreached peoples. Adopt a group for specific prayer.
- Ask the Lord how He wants you to be involved in reaching "your" group.

My prayer is that the "Lord of the Harvest" will "thrust forth laborers" into that part of the Harvest that includes "your" people group.

—Allen Starling
Gospel Recordings

Beyond personal support needs, profits from this book go to The Bozo Fund.

Although the authors acknowledge many bozos in their own culture, the Bozos to be benefitted by sale of *Catch the Vision 2000* are an unreached people group of Mali in West Africa. The Bozo Fund sponsors research and church-planting efforts among this group.

There *will* be Bozos in heaven, since gathered before the throne of the Lamb are men Christ has purchased with His blood from "every tribe and tongue and people and nation" (Revelation 5:9). So reaching the Bozos is only a matter of when and by whom.

Perhaps you're part of God's plan to reach the Bozos. Contact your mission agency or:

> Bill and Amy Stearns
> PO Box 416
> Colorado Springs, CO 80901-0416